GOOD HOUSEKEEPING

How to Remove
STAINS

PRACTICAL · GH · LIBRARY

GOOD HOUSEKEEPING

How to Remove

STAINS

The comprehensive guide to

- Dealing with every household stain from adhesives to wine

- Choosing the right solvent for the job

- Laundering every kind of fabric

- Cleaning restoring and caring for every type of surface

PLUS Where to buy specialized cleaners
Where to buy what the professionals use

EBURY PRESS LONDON

Published by Ebury Press
Division of The National Magazine Company Ltd
Colquhoun House
27–37 Broadwick Street
London W1V 1FR

First impression 1988

The Good Housekeeping Institute is the food and consumer
research centre of *Good Housekeeping* Magazine

Text by Cassandra Kent
Consumer Affairs Editor
Good Housekeeping, Magazine
Research and revision by Gillian Smedley
Director of Communications, Good Housekeeping Institute
Designed by Gwyn Lewis
Cartoons by Robert Bloomfield

Typeset by Textype Typesetters, Cambridge

Printed and bound in Great Britain by Mackays of Chatham PLC, Kent

Contents

Introduction   7

Part 1   Types of stain – and the solvent to use   11

Part 2   A–Z of Stain Removal   19

Part 3   Surfaces – and how to care for them   62

Part 4   Fabric laundering guide   131

Addresses   136

Index   140

Acknowledgements

We wish to thank the following organizations for their help in compiling this book.

BAYER (UK) Fibres Division LTD
THE BOOTS COMPANY PLC NOTTINGHAM ENGLAND
BRICK DEVELOPMENT ASSOCIATION
BRITISH CARPET MANUFACTURERS' ASSOCIATION LTD
BRITISH MAN-MADE FIBRES FEDERATION
COURTAULDS PLC
THE FABRIC CARE RESEARCH ASSOCIATION
FURNITURE INDUSTRY RESEARCH ASSOCIATION
HOME LAUNDERING CONSULATATIVE COUNCIL
ICI FIBRES
INTERNATIONAL WOOL SECRETARIAT
LEVER BROTHERS LTD
THE JOHN LEWIS PARTNERSHIP
OPTICAL INFORMATION COUNCIL
PROCTER & GAMBLE LTD
VICTORIA AND ALBERT MUSEUM

We would like to express our thanks to the staff at the Good Housekeeping Institute for their combined expertise and experience which has made this book possible.

Metric measurements:

In accordance with metric development, spoon measurements in this book are given in millilitres. If you do not have a set of metric measuring spoons the conversion is as follows:

1 teaspoon	5 ml
1 tablespoon	15 ml

Introduction

This is the book that no home should be without. Whether you lead a life of pristine perfection or muddling-through chaos, things will get spilled — some day, somewhere. This book tells you how to get the marks out, how to treat the different materials which are affected and how to keep all household surfaces in the best possible condition.

The expertise in the book is distilled from years of practical work by the Good Housekeeping Institute. Stains have been removed in the course of preparing articles for *Good Housekeeping* magazine, as a result of letters from desperate readers and in a spirit of enquiry as new stain removal products come onto the market.

This book doesn't pull punches. It tells you if you're likely to be stuck with a stain forever; when you'd be a fool to attempt treatment yourself; and when you must decide if treatment's a risk worth taking. Unlike many books of its type, *Good Housekeeping How to Remove Stains* names products with branded examples. So you, the user, don't have to work out what a proprietary grease solvent is. You can go into a shop and ask for it by name.

The first edition of this book was reprinted seven times. This new revised edition takes account of developments in stain removal technology and the latest products. Where the old methods are best, it tells you so. Where new products excel, you'll find information on them.

The alphabetical list of stains and surfaces makes it quick and easy to look up what you need to know. Keep this book somewhere you can lay your hands on it easily. It's an investment which could save you pounds.

Cassandra Kent
Consumer Affairs Editor
Good Housekeeping

WARNING

Many stain removing agents, including proprietary products, are potentially harmful if not actually poisonous. Some are highly flammable; others give off toxic fumes. The sensible course of action is to treat all stain removing substances with caution and in the case of proprietary products, go by the manufacturer's directions scrupulously. Follow these simple rules as a routine measure.

When using:

Always work in a well-ventilated room, preferably with a window open. Never use stain removing agents in a room where there is a naked flame, pilot light or radiant heater. Never smoke while working with, or anywhere near to, stain removing agents. Do not decant any solvent into another container. Wear household gloves.

When storing:

Keep all items in your stain removing kit out of the reach of children or elderly people whose sight is failing, or who may become confused; best of all, keep your kit locked away. Never put away anything that is not clearly labelled. Store – and indeed buy – only small quantities of stain removing substances. Take extra precautions when using or handling the following:

Methylated spirit	Highly flammable and poisonous
Spirits of salts	Poisonous and corrosive
Amyl acetate Liquid lighter fuel Turpentine White spirit, or turpentine substitute Non-oily nail varnish remover Cellulose thinners	Flammable and dangerous to inhale; poisonous
Ammonia	Unpleasant fumes; avoid contact with eyes, skin or clothing; poisonous

Note: The Good Housekeeping Institute in this book recommends only aerosol products which are free from chlorofluorocarbons (CFCs) and which should not damage the ozone layer.

How to use this book

Part 1: *Types of Stain – and the solvent to use*, gives you essential background information on stain removal, together with details of useful items to include in your stain removal kit.

To deal with a particular stain – say, cod liver oil – turn to *Part 2: A–Z of Stain Removal*, and look up COD LIVER OIL. Under this entry you will find a number of sub-headings, from *on carpets* to *on woollen clothes*, telling you exactly what to do.

If, however, your problem is one of general cleaning and care (say, your sisal matting is looking grubby, or you'd like advice on caring for a tortoiseshell-backed hair brush) turn to *Part 3: Surfaces – and how to care for them*. You will find the answer under SISAL MATTING or TORTOISESHELL.

For burns, dents, scratches, eg on furniture, again *see* PART 3, under FURNITURE.

The advice given in this book is based on research and practical work carried out by Good Housekeeping Institute. However, an initial test should always be undertaken on the item involved as GHI can accept no responsiblity for any damage or loss that might ensue from following the methods suggested.

1

Types of stain – and the solvent to use

Spills occur in even the best-run homes – and they're not just caused by high-spirited children or bouncy pets knocking over flower vases. Everyone has 'off' days when they drop things – an unexpected noise can cause an otherwise steady hand to falter, a minute's delay can mean a burn mark on a saucepan. Then there are the stains that creep up on a home unaided by human hand. Things like mildew on shower curtains or leather-bound books, fly specks on fabric lampshades and soot marks on brickwork.

However, with a little knowledge, speed and care, most stains *can* be removed – often leaving no trace and almost always producing a distinct improvement on the stain mark itself. In this book we tell you how to deal with (almost) all household stains yourself from both the point of view of the stains and the surfaces on which they occur. So whether you've spilled an entire bottle of ink on your best rug or bought a house where the carpets look as if unmentionable deeds have been perpetrated on them, read on.

General points on stain removal

As a general rule, it's much easier to remove any stain if you *treat it as soon as it occurs* or, at any rate, as soon as you realize it's occurred. The occasion when you shouldn't do this is when the particular stain, or surface on which it has fallen, requires professional treatment. We tell you when it's safe to do it yourself or when you should get professional help.

Before treating any stain you must consider three things: the stain itself, the surface on which it is, and any special dye, treatment or finish on that surface. It is essential, whatever method of removal you adopt – be it cold water or a proprietary cleaner – to *test it first* on a small, hidden area of the surface. This need take no more than a minute or so and could prevent you ruining something irrevocably. Even if you're sure that you know what product gets what stain out of what surface, it may be that there is some additional unknown factor present in what you are treating, so a test run is vital.

There are a number of quick first-aid treatments which can be applied to certain things and are useful if, for example, you are in mid-dinner party or meeting and don't feel able to stop and administer thorough stain removal treatment on the spot. Non-greasy stains can be sponged or rinsed through with cold water. Greasy ones can be sprinkled with talcum powder to stop them spreading. On tablecloths, salt thrown on to wine, fruit or beetroot stains will stop them spreading. Salt should *not* be thrown on to carpets as it tends to affect colours and to leave a damp patch which will attract moisture and make them soil more readily.

One golden rule is to *go cautiously* when treating stains. Milder methods repeated as often as necessary are far more effective than a blast from a strong solvent which is as likely to damage the surface as to get out the stain.

Bear in mind that a stain has fallen *on* to something and therefore needs to be taken *off* it. When applying a solvent to an absorbed stain (*see* STAINS DEFINED) that hasn't responded to sponging or laundering, work from the side underneath the stain, holding a dry, white absorbent pad on the other side. A built-up stain (*see* STAINS DEFINED) should, where possible, be treated from the underside with a pad held on top of the mark so that the deposit is not driven through the fabric. Any absorbent pad used in these ways should be moved around continually to prevent any of the stain being re-deposited on the surface.

How to tackle a stain

When treating any stain, treat a ring around the stain and then *work from the outside to the middle*; this prevents it from spreading. It is also important to dab at a stain rather than rub it as rubbing may both spread the stain and damage the surface. Where removing a stain has left an amazingly clean spot on something, launder or have it dry-cleaned immediately. Always *use white absorbent cotton cloth* or cotton-wool as a dabber for any solvent or treatment. A coloured fabric dabber may have its dyes affected by certain solvents and cause you to end up with two stains, rather than one, on the original surface.

Professional cleaning is a must if a difficult stain has fallen on to an expensive garment or piece of soft furnishing. Although it's expensive it will certainly pay off in terms of saving the item from permanent marking. Professional dry-cleaners have a battery of cleaning solvents not available on the domestic market and should be able to deal with the most obstinate stains. It is best not to attempt home treatment first as this can complicate and sometimes spoil their work. Be sure to tell them exactly what has been spilled and also to confess if you have had a go at removing it yourself, saying what you used. It is often a help for professional cleaners if you mark round the edge of the stain with tacking stitches – though obviously not on a fabric such as silk where the stitch marks would show.

Stains defined

For home removal purposes, stains can be divided into three groups as follows:

Absorbed stains   These are spilled liquids, eg tea, coffee, milk or beer, which have been absorbed into a surface. Provided they are treated when they occur, it is usually possible simply to rinse them out of washable fabrics, using lukewarm suds and gently squeezing and rubbing the stained section, fabric to fabric. It is important not to use hot water, which could set the stain. Where you cannot wash an article immediately, leave it soaking in cold water until you can. *Don't* soak wool, silk or any fabric with a flame-resistant finish.

After rubbing the stain in suds, laundering at the temperature recommended for the fabric is usually sufficient to clear any remaining traces. At any rate try this before attacking the traces of stain with a commercial stain remover or a bleach. Immediate use of clear lukewarm water is also the safest way of treating absorbed stains on fabrics which are normally dry-cleaned, provided the fabric is not the type which watermarks. Sponge the stain gently, then blot well with a clean white cloth or unpatterned kitchen paper towel.

Built-up stains   These are made by thicker preparations such as grease, nail varnish and paint. They leave a surface deposit but do not generally penetrate far into a surface. The more quickly you can treat them, the less likely they are to set and perhaps cause damage to the surface below. Use paper tissues, towels or a suitable tool such as a metal ruler or back of a knife blade to remove as much of the deposit as possible. Treat any remaining stain according to what caused it (*see* PART 2). Follow treatment by laundering or sponging where necessary.

Compound stains   These are caused by substances such as blood which produce a combination of the two types of stain already mentioned, ie they penetrate a surface and leave some residue on top. First the deposit should be treated as in built-up stains, then the penetration should be attended to as in absorbed stains. Final laundering or sponging will almost certainly be needed to clear any remaining traces.

OTHER TYPES OF STAIN

Dried and set stains Start with a mild method of removal and, if this fails, move on to something stronger. PART 2 gives details of what to use on what mark. Keep a note of what has been used in what order, in case you have finally to resort to the services of a dry-cleaner.

Mystery stains on fabrics Be very careful with unidentified stains. On washables, soak where possible and then launder. With non-washables, sponge the stained area with clear lukewarm water after testing on an inconspicuous section and pressing out the moisture in a towel if you think the fabric might watermark. Treat obvious grease marks with a grease solvent. Stains that persist can, on washables, be treated with diluted hydrogen peroxide and, on non-washables, with diluted ammonia. Watch carefully to check that colour is not affected by this. If it is or if the stains persist despite treatment, seek professional help.

Stain removal on upholstery Don't over-wet upholstered furniture. It helps to blot up with an old white towel as you go along to avoid this. Be particularly careful not to over-wet acrylic velvet, eg Dralon, which is woven on to a cotton or cotton/synthetic mixture backing which could shrink and distort the surface.

Water-borne stains can often be removed from Dralon velvet and from non-removable flat-weave Dralon covers by immediate and thorough blotting followed, where necessary, by sprinkling the stain with a weak, warm solution of enzyme detergent (15ml detergent per litre water) and lightly wiping the way of the pile with a clean sponge. Velvets other than acrylic, and any brocatelles, should be handled professionally. Some dry-cleaners are prepared to come and treat upholstery in your home which, although an expensive service, could work out cheaper than taking your three-piece suite to them.

Stain removal on carpets A squirt from a soda syphon will flush out spilled liquids if used immediately the spill occurs. Remember to keep the syphon always full. Dirty marks and water-soluble stains can be removed usually with carpet shampoo, used according to the manufacturer's instructions. Having treated the stain itself with carpet shampoo, it may be necessary to shampoo the whole carpet to avoid a patch showing. Any stain which persists should be treated according to type (*see* PART 2) or professional help must be called in.

When shampooing the stain, mop with an old white towel as you go to avoid over-wetting. Where a carpet can be raised, treat the back as well, but take great care with solvents on rubber-latexed or foam-backed carpets.

Following treatment, smooth the carpet pile in the direction in which it lies and allow it to dry naturally (don't apply artificial heat from a hair dryer, for example, which can damage it) before replacing the furniture.

For water-based stains when you've run out of carpet shampoo, use a solution of 5ml delicate fabric detergent and 5ml white vinegar to 500ml of warm water.

The stain remover's kit

While a stain removal kit, permanently at the ready in your home, can save a lot of money, time and temper, it is important to bear in mind that the majority of items in it are **poisonous**. It should therefore be kept out of the reach of children, preferably locked away. Be sure that all the items in it are labelled clearly. Do not decant anything into another container such as a squash bottle. Most stain removers are used only in small quantities at a time so there is no need to indulge in bulk buying of any item. Little and often is a more sensible solution.

As we have stressed in the warning note at the beginning of the book, certain solvents which are virtually indispensable in stain removal are **flammable**, while some give off toxic vapours. If possible always open a window in the room where you are using them, or at any rate leave the door open. Wear rubber gloves to avoid any damage to your hands and **never, ever smoke or use solvents in a room where an open fire or radiant heater is burning. Turn off any pilot lights**.

Here is a list of the most useful items to have handy. You may in fact keep a number of them for purposes other than stain removal. It would nonetheless be sensible to invest in a small, additional container of each to keep in your stain removal box. Otherwise you may be sure that the day you need nail varnish remover to get out clear adhesive from a child's cotton shirt will be the day before you planned to buy a new bottle for your dressing table.

Ammonia   Household ammonia will remove certain stains and is also good for neutralizing acid marks. It should be used diluted in cold water as recommended, always in a well-ventilated room as it gives off unpleasant fumes. Ammonia can cause certain types of dye to bleed so should be tested carefully on coloured fabrics. *Avoid contact with skin, eyes and clothing.*

Enzyme (biological) wash powder This type of detergent is much better than the ordinary kind on protein stains such as blood, egg yolk, milk, gravy and perspiration, where a pre-wash soaking is useful. You should always follow any instructions on length of soak and temperature of water provided by the manufacturer. Make sure the powder is thoroughly dissolved before immersing the article. Enzyme detergent should not be used on protein fibres such as wool or silk, nor on non-colourfast, flame-resistant or rubberized fabrics. It should not be used to soak any item with metal fastenings. When soaking colourfast articles make sure the whole article is immersed in case there is a slight colour change.

Glycerine This is useful for lubricating and softening staining substances on any fabric and colour. A soft stain is always easier to remove by the appropriate method than one that has set hard. Use glycerine diluted in equal parts with warm water. Rub it into the fabric and leave for one hour. Remove by rinsing or sponging with lukewarm water.

Grease solvents Proprietary grease solvents – hereafter called stain removers – remove grease and oil marks and some will also cope with other stains. Check and follow the manufacturer's instructions exactly. Stain removers may be liquid or aerosol. Good ones include Beaucaire, Thawpit, Dabitoff, Stain Devils and The Stain Slayer liquids, Goddard's Dry Clean, Boots Dry Cleaner Spray Stain Remover and K2R Stain Remover Spray aerosols (the last can also be used on wallpaper and stone). All should be used in a well-ventilated room. *Avoid smoking* and excessive inhalation of the vapour. Also avoid excessive contact with the skin or with plastic objects and surfaces. Aerosols must be applied from the recommended distance; any closer and they cause ring marking.

Hydrogen peroxide This is available from chemists and is a mild slow-acting, oxidizing bleach. Buy it in 20 vol strength and use it diluted with 1 part to 6 parts of cold water. It should not be used on nylon or flame-resistant fabrics, but most other fabrics, including silk, can be soaked in the solution for up to 30 minutes, though you should bear in mind that it will have a slow, overall bleaching action on coloured fabrics. (White articles can be soaked overnight if necessary.) To speed the stain removal process on coloureds you can add 2.5ml ammonia to each litre of hydrogen peroxide and water solution but never add ammonia when the fabric is or contains wool.

Laundry or domestic borax This is a mild alkali which works on acid stains.

Borax is usually used in a solution of 15ml to 500ml warm water for sponging or for soaking washable fabrics (10–15 minutes should do the trick). Note that soaking coloured fabrics for any longer could result in slight, overall bleaching. On white fabrics, sprinkle laundry borax directly on to the dampened stain. Stretch the fabric over a basin and pour hot water through the stain until it disappears. The big advantage of laundry borax is that it can be used safely on most fabrics.

Methylated spirit An excellent stain-removing solvent, though note that it is *highly flammable and poisonous*. Use it neat, dabbed on to the stain, but check first that colour will not be affected. Methylated spirit should never be used on acetate or triacetate fabrics or on French-polished surfaces where it will dissolve the polish.

White vinegar or dilute acetic acid Both are useful on certain stains and both should be thoroughly rinsed out of fabrics. Never use them on acetate or triacetate fabrics. Take care not to get acetic acid on your skin. Acetic acid can cause dye bleeding so test carefully.

Other solvents Other useful solvents to keep in your kit – nearly all *flammable and dangerous to inhale* – are amyl acetate, white spirit or turpentine substitute, liquid lighter fuel, non-oily nail varnish remover (don't use on acetate or triacetate fabrics), cellulose thinners.

Pre-wash laundry aids These are available for use on heavily soiled and stained areas on washable white and colourfast fabrics; three examples are Frend (trigger spray), Shout (aerosol) and Vanish (stain removing bar). They break down most types of staining matter and loosen ingrained grime so that the residue can then be washed out by the normal laundering process. This eliminates the need for pre-soaking, hard rubbing or scrubbing and boiling.

The spray and aerosol should be used on dry fabric, and the bar rubbed on to dampened fabric immediately before laundering. They work best on grease-based soiling and fresh stains; stubborn marks may require two or three treatments. They are not effective on dye staining, paint, permanent ink, rust or blood, although they sometimes effect a slight improvement on old blood stains.

Proprietary kits It is possible to buy kits designed to cope with most household stains. They usually contain a number of small bottles of different chemicals which you use individually or mix together according to the stain. A good one is the ServiceMaster

First Aid Kit for carpets, rugs and furniture. Other specialized kits are referred to in PART 2 under the particular stain which they remove. For information on where to obtain kits and products that are not readily available in the shops *see* ADDRESSES page 136.

2

A–Z of Stain Removal

Adhesives

Scrape off the deposit then treat as follows according to type.

GENERAL NOTE ON ADHESIVES

A number of manufacturers are aware of the problems caused by staining and have formulated their own solvents. These are not normally sold in shops but have to be obtained direct from the manufacturers. You may feel that for the odd gluing job it is not worth obtaining a special solvent but if you are embarking on major DIY work involving adhesives or if your children are keen on making models, it would be sensible to invest in a supply of the appropriate solvent.

Clear adhesive eg Bostik No. 1

on carpets Dab any stain lightly with a pad and non-oily nail varnish remover. If you're not sure what the pile is made of, use amyl acetate but check first for dye bleeding. (*See* page 11.)
on clothes and upholstery Hold an absorbent pad on the right side. From the wrong side dab with a pad and non-oily nail varnish remover. On acetate and triacetate use amyl acetate but check first for dye bleeding.

Contact adhesive eg Evo-Stik

on carpets Speed is essential as it is virtually impossible to remove this type of adhesive once it has hardened. Evo-Stik Adhesive Cleaner (191) will dilute the adhesive while in its wet state so it can be wiped clear (*see* ADDRESSES). Follow the manufacturer's instruction and test first on a hidden section.
on clothes and upholstery Treatment as for carpets.

Epoxy Resin eg Araldite

on carpets Dab with cellulose thinners. On a synthetic pile carpet or a synthetic fibre mixture use lighter fuel. Dried stains will be impossible to remove but trimming the pile with sharp scissors will often remove a light surface deposit.
on clothes and upholstery Hold a pad over the deposit. Dab from

the wrong side with cellulose thinners. On synthetic fibres use lighter fuel. Stains that have dried will be impossible to remove.

Sticky label backing and adhesive tape residue

on china, glass and vitreous enamel When a label cannot be peeled off, soak or rub with a damp cloth. If this fails, use Mangers De-Solv-it or rub with white spirit, methylated spirit or cellulose thinners. Do a test area first. Following treatment, wipe surface with a damp cloth or wash the item if possible.

on metals Clear residue with amyl acetate, nail varnish remover or Mangers De-Solv-it and wipe down and dry the surface.

on fabrics Stain Devils Glue & Chewing Gum Stain Remover will clear residue from adhesive labels.

Latex adhesive eg Copydex

on carpets Clear as much as possible with a dry cloth before it hardens, then trickle on cold water to keep it soft and rub with a cloth. When dry, treat any residual stain with a liquid dry cleaner e.g. Dabitoff. Loosen dried stains with a pencil rubber and use Dabitoff.

on clothes and upholstery While still wet, this can be removed with a damp cloth. Where possible, soak the area in cold water and rub vigorously. Once dry, scrape off the deposit and dab the remaining stain with Dabitoff stain remover.

on hard surfaces Gentle rubbing with a clean fingertip will usually roll off latex adhesive, unless it has been allowed to set for some time. On stubborn stains use Mangers De-Solv-it after testing on a hidden area.

Model-making cement eg Humbrol Polystyrene Cement

on carpets, clothing and upholstery Wipe off as much as possible, taking care not to spread the adhesive. Dab the remainder with a pad well moistened with liquid stain remover. Once dried, the cement is extremely difficult to remove but some manufacturers produce a solvent for this (*see* ADDRESSES).

Alcohol *see* BEER; GIN AND OTHER SPIRITS; WINE.

on wood see PART 3, FURNITURE, REMOVING MARKS.

Animal stains

blood see BLOOD.

excreta/sick on carpets Speed is essential to prevent permanent

staining and odour. Remove deposit with absorbent paper or a spoon. Flush the area with a squirt from a soda syphon or sponge with clear, warm water. Blot dry. Use a proprietary pet stain remover to clear and deodorize the area, eg Shaws No-Stain, Bissell 'Not on the Carpet' Accident Cleaner. If you have a pet stain remover already in the house, use it initially, according to the manufacturer's instructions. Finally shampoo the carpet if necessary. Blot well. (Note that dried matter can sometimes be softened for easier removal by using a proprietary pet stain remover.) Shaws Pet Stain Remover can also be used on linoleum tiles, other floor areas and pet living quarters.

urine/sick on bedcovers, cushions and upholstery Act quickly to lessen penetration. Remove any deposit with absorbent paper, taking care not to spread the mark. Blot dry. If it is not possible to remove the item, try to isolate the affected area by gathering up the fabric and tying white tape or string tightly round it. Rinse under cold running water if possible, or use a pet stain remover, eg Shaws No-Stain can also be used on linoleum, tiles, other floor areas and pet living quarters.

urine on carpet Speed is essential to prevent bleaching. Blot up the excess and flush the area with a squirt from a soda syphon or sponge with warm water. Blot well. Shampoo the carpet. Bissell Carpet Shampoo contains a deodorizer. Alternatively use a pet stain remover, eg Shaws No-Stain, Bissell 'Not on the Carpet' Accident Cleaner as directed.

Artists' paints

Oil and alkyd colours can be cleared from brushes and hands with Artgel. Artwipes can also be used on hands and painting accessories.

acrylic paint on clothing If still wet, blot off excess paint with absorbent paper and wash out with soap and water. If a stain has dried, place an absorbent pad under it, if possible, and dab the stain with cotton-wool moistened with a liquid stain remover, eg Beaucaire, methylated spirit or Winsol Paint Remover and Solvent (*see* ADDRESSES). Check that the product can be used on the fabric involved. It is particularly important to do a test area on synthetics. Note that it may not be possible to remove all the colour where a stain has dried completely.

oil paint on clothing Hold an absorbent pad under the stain. Dab the right side with white spirit. Sponge or launder. Where the paint has hardened, use a liquid stain remover such as Beaucaire, Stain Devils Tar & Paint Stain Remover or Winsol Paint Remover and Solvent (*see* ADDRESSES). Check that the product can be used on the fabric involved. It is particularly important to do a test area on synthetics.

poster, powder and water-colour paint on clothes Sponge well with cold water. If necessary leave to soak in cold water. Launder to remove any remaining traces or use methylated spirit for this.

Ballpoint ink stains *see* INK

Bath stains

For marks on vitreous or porcelain enamelled baths, *see* below: on plastic baths *see* PART 3, BATHS.

blue/green drip stains   Use a proprietary vitreous enamel cleaner recommended by the Vitreous Enamel Development Council for 'bath' or 'general' use (*see* ADDRESSES). On no account use vinegar or any other acid for this purpose as it can damage the glaze.

hard water marks   White deposits around taps and waste outlet can be removed as above. Rinse well. Stubborn marks may need a second treatment or the use of Oz Bath Cleaner (not on Vogue baths), the cream cleaner Celmac RB90, or Jenolite Bath Stain Remover. Test on a hidden area.

neglected stains   These can usually be removed with Oz Bath Cleaner or specially formulated chemical treatment for sanitary-ware, eg Celmac Liftoff Stain and Scale Remover. Follow the manufacturer's directions carefully or you may damage the surface of the bath. Train your household to rinse the bath after use to ensure that neglected stains do not occur in future.

rust marks   If treatment as for drip stains does not remove rust marks, use a proprietary cleaner with rust-removing properties, eg Jenolite Bath Stain Remover (*see* ADDRESSES). Follow the manufacturer's directions carefully and neutralize with the recommended solvent (usually water).

tide marks   Where these do not respond to the treatment given for drip stains, rub with a cloth moistened in white spirit. Wash off immediately with a solution of washing-up liquid and rinse thoroughly. Avoid repetition by encouraging users to clean the bath after each use.

Beer

on carpets   Flush fresh stains with a squirt from a soda syphon or sponge with clear warm water. Blot well. Treat any remaining stain or dried marks with a carpet shampoo, such as the trigger dispensed foam 1001 Troubleshooter. Alternatively use a proprietary spotting kit, eg ServiceMaster First Aid Kit or Greendale Carpet and Fabric Spot'N'Stain Removal Kit (*see* ADDRESSES). Gentle sponging with methylated spirit may reduce old stains.

on table linen and washable fabrics   Rinse through or soak fresh stains in lukewarm water. Launder as usual. For dried stains on white cottons and linen, launder first then bleach out any remaining stain with a hydrogen peroxide solution (1 part 20 vol hydrogen peroxide to 6 parts cold water). On coloured fabrics (not acetate or triacetate) sponge with a white vinegar solution (30ml vinegar to 500ml water). On acetate and triacetate, sponge with a laundry borax solution (15ml borax to 500ml warm water). Launder.

on upholstery and non-washable fabrics   Blot well and wipe with a cloth wrung out in clear, lukewarm water. Dried stains on non-acetate/triacetate fabrics should be sponged carefully with a white vinegar solution (1 part white vinegar to 5 parts water) and then with clear water. Blot well. Alternatively, and for acetate or triacetate fabrics, sponge with clear water, allow to dry naturally, and treat with a proprietary aerosol cleaner such as K2R Stain Remover Spray or Goddard's Dry Clean. On upholstery, a spotting kit (*see* BEER ON CARPETS) can be used.

Beetroot Juice

on table linen   Rinse immediately in cold water. Use laundry borax in solution (15ml borax to 500ml warm water) for soaking coloureds. For whites, sprinkle borax in powder form on the dampened stain, then stretch over a basin and pour boiling water through. Soaking and laundering in an enzyme detergent solution is also effective. Dried stains on white fabrics should respond to the use of Stain Devils Fruit & Wine Stain Remover.

Bird droppings

on carpets   Wipe or brush up the surface deposit and sponge with warm water. If necessary sponge with a laundry borax solution (15ml borax to 500ml warm water). Rinse and blot dry. Treat stubborn marks with a proprietary stain remover, eg Bissell 'Not on the Carpet' Accident Cleaner.

on non-washable fabrics and upholstery   Wipe or brush up the deposit. Use repeated applications of an aerosol stain remover, eg Goddard's Dry Clean, until clear.

on washing on the line   Further laundering should remove most stains although it may be necessary to use careful hydrogen peroxide bleaching (1 part 20 vol peroxide to 6 parts cold water) for white and colourfast fabrics (other than nylon) if the bird has been eating berries. A dilute solution of a proprietary bleach, eg Domestos, can be used on white cottons and linens but not on wool, silk, crease-resistant, drip-dry, embossed or piqué fabrics.

Blackberry *see* FRUIT JUICE.

Blackcurrant *see* FRUIT JUICE.

Blood

on bed sheets and washable fabrics　Fresh bloodstains should be sponged immediately with cold salt water, then soaked in a warm enzyme detergent solution according to the maker's directions. Launder in warm suds. Dried stains which do not respond to an enzyme soak may need further soaking in a hydrogen peroxide solution (1 part 20 vol hydrogen peroxide to 6 parts cold water) with added ammonia (2.5ml ammonia to every 1 litre solution). Don't use hydrogen peroxide on nylon. Rinse well. Stain Devils Blood & Milk Stain Remover will usually clear this stain and should be used prior to laundering.

on carpets　Flush out fresh stains with a squirt from a soda syphon, or sponge well with cold water. Blot dry. If necessary, shampoo area. Alternatively use a proprietary carpet spotting kit. Professional cleaning may be necessary to clear dried stains.

on mattresses　Small areas of fresh staining may respond to an application of a thick, barely-moistened paste of bicarbonate of soda and water. Press on and leave until dry. Brush clear. For larger stains, tip the mattress on to its side to lessen penetration and, holding a towel beneath the stained area to avoid spreading the mark, sponge with cold salt water, then clear cold water. Blot thoroughly. The lather from an upholstery shampoo is usually effective on fresh marks and may also clear dried stains. Treating mattress stains is done more easily by two people – one to hold and one to dab. Mattress covers may ring mark but this is preferable to an untreated stain.

on non-washable fabrics and upholstery　Wipe or brush lightly to remove any surface deposit. Sponge with cold water to which you have added a few drops of ammonia (2.5ml to every 1 litre). Rinse with clean water and blot well. Alternatively use an upholstery spotting kit (*see* ADDRESSES).

Bottled sauces *see* KETCHUP AND BOTTLED SAUCES.

Brandy *see* GIN AND OTHER SPIRITS.

Bruise marks

on wood see PART 3, FURNITURE, REMOVING MARKS.

Burns

on wood see PART 3, FURNITURE, REMOVING MARKS.

Butter *see* FATS, GREASE AND OILS.

Candle wax

on carpets   Scrape off as much as possible of the deposit with the bowl of a spoon. To melt the remainder, place a sheet of blotting paper or brown paper over it and gently apply the toe of a warm iron to the mark. Do not let the iron touch the pile, which would probably scorch or melt, and keep moving the paper around until all the wax is absorbed. Clear remaining wax with a stain remover, eg Mangers De-Solv-it, Dabitoff. Remove any remaining colour by dabbing with methylated spirit.

on polished wood surfaces   Hold a plastic bag of ice cubes over the wax to harden it thoroughly. Chip at it carefully with a fingernail or plastic spatula. When all deposit is gone, rub with a duster to remove any film. Polish with your usual polish. Where heat marking has occurred, rub hard along the grain with a cloth dipped in a traditional cream metal polish. Hold it over just one finger so that you do not cover an area larger than the mark.

on table linen and washable fabrics   Remove surface deposit with a fingernail, taking care not to snag the fabric. Place clean white blotting paper both sides of the stain and melt out any remaining wax with a warm iron. Keep moving the paper around for maximum absorption. Apply a stain remover, eg Mangers De-Solv-it, to clear remaining traces of wax. Launder to clear any remaining colour left by a coloured candle.

on upholstery fabrics   On closely woven fabrics melt out the wax with a moderately hot iron over clean white blotting paper. Remove any remaining colour mark by dabbing with methylated spirit (not on acetate or triacetate). On loosely woven fabrics do not attempt to pull off any wax or you may pull threads. Melt it out with an iron and blotting paper. Remove colour traces with methylated spirit. On pile fabrics it is often possible to remove the deposit by rubbing lightly with a cloth. Otherwise use the iron and blotting paper treatment with blotting paper on the pile side and the iron applied to the back. Where this is not possible hold the iron over the blotting paper but without depressing the pile. Clear any wax with an aerosol stain remover, eg Goddard's Dry Clean.

on vinyl wall coverings   Wait until the wax hardens then lift it off carefully, dabbing gently with methylated spirit on a cotton wool bud to remove any dye left. A liquid householder cleaner, eg Handy Andy, should remove any slight stain remaining.

on wallpaper Do not attempt to lift the wax or scrape the paper which will tear away leaving holes. Use a warm iron over a sheet of blotting paper to melt and absorb the wax. Keep moving the blotting paper around to expose clear surfaces. If a stain remains use an aerosol stain remover, eg K2R Stain Remover Spray. Sometimes it may not be possible to remove all traces.

Car and cycle oil

on drives and garage floors Use Mangers De-Solv-it on concrete, Mangers Sugar Soap for asphalt surfaces (*see* ADDRESSES). Betterware Oil Patch Remover can be used on both surfaces, as well as on stone and wood.

on fabrics *see* FATS, GREASE AND OILS.

Carbon paper

on fabrics Dab the mark lightly with a pad of cotton-wool moistened with methylated spirit. Alternatively, and on acetate and triacetate, use K2R Stain Remover Spray.

Chewing gum

on carpets Use Mangers De-Solv-it (*see* ADDRESSES). Follow the maker's instructions, test an area first. Alternatively use the liquid cleaner Keyline Chewing Gum Remover following the instructions.

on jerseys, worsted trousers, nylon playsuits Place the article in the refrigerator or hold a plastic bag of ice cubes over the deposit to harden it so that it can be cracked and picked off. Any remaining deposit can be removed by a liquid stain remover such as The Stain Slayer, Keyline Chewing Gum Remover (both also safe for use on hair), egg white or Swarfega Hand Cleanser rubbed in gently but persistently until the gum dissolves. Launder where possible or sponge the treated area with warm water.

on upholstery Use Mangers De-Solv-it (*see* ADDRESSES).

Chocolate

on bed linen and washable fabrics Scrape off any deposit with the back of a knife blade. Soak, then launder at the temperature recommended for the fabric, using an enzyme detergent if suitable. If stain remains, sprinkle the wet mark with laundry borax powder, stretch the fabric over a basin and pour hot water through. Rinse. Alternatively, use a stain remover such as Beaucaire, Dabitoff or Stain Devils Ball Point Pen Stain Remover.

on carpets   Scrape off as much as possible with a blunt knife. Treat the stained area with carpet shampoo. Treat any remaining stain with a liquid stain remover, eg Beaucaire (not on foam backed carpets).

on non-washable fabrics   Scrape off any deposit with the back of a knife blade. Use a proprietary stain remover such as Beaucaire or aerosol Dabitoff.

Chutney *see* JAM.

Cocoa

on carpets   Spoon and blot up as much as possible. Flush out the stain with a squirt from a soda syphon or sponge with warm water. Blot well. Use a carpet shampoo or a carpet spotting kit (*see* ADDRESSES). When dry, remove any traces with a liquid stain remover eg Beaucaire (not on foam backed carpets). Dried stains should be sponged well with a laundry borax solution (15ml borax to 500ml warm water). Blot dry and if a mark remains, rub in a mixture of equal parts of glycerine and warm water. Leave for up to an hour then sponge with cold water and blot. A dry foam carpet shampoo should clear any remaining stain. Repeat the glycerine treatment if necessary.

on non-washable fabrics and upholstery Sponge with a laundry borax solution (15ml borax to 500ml warm water) then with clear water blotting frequently to avoid over-wetting. Blot dry. Clear any traces when dry by applying an aerosol stain remover, eg Goddard's Dry Clean. Alternatively use an upholstery spotting kit (*see* ADDRESSES).

on table linen and washable fabrics Rinse thoroughly in warm water. Soak in a warm enzyme detergent solution if the fabric is suitable, or use Vanish stain removing bar. Launder in hand-hot suds. When dry, use a stain remover to remove any traces, eg Beaucaire, Dabitoff. Stubborn marks on white cottons and linens may respond to treatment with a bleach solution but do not use on crease-resistant, drip-dry, embossed or piqué fabrics.

Cod liver oil

on carpets Spoon or blot up the excess and treat with a suitable stain remover, eg Mangers De-Solv-it. Follow with a dry foam carpet shampoo, eg Bissell, and avoid over-wetting. Alternatively, use a carpet spotting kit eg Bissell. With heavy spillage, it may be necessary to treat the stain again after a few days as the oil 'wicks' back.

on non-washable fabrics Dab with a liquid stain remover, eg The Stain Slayer. On fabrics likely to ring mark use an aerosol stain remover, eg Goddard's Dry Clean.

on washable fabrics Before the stain has a chance to dry, launder the garment in a synthetic detergent solution as hot as the fabric will take. Treat dried stains with a liquid stain remover, eg Thawpit, Stain Devils Grease & Oil Stain Remover, then lubricate any remaining marks with a glycerine solution (equal parts glycerine and warm water) and leave for up to an hour before rinsing in clear water followed by laundering. Stubborn marks (not on nylon) may need bleaching out with a hydrogen peroxide solution (1 part 20 vol peroxide to 6 parts cold water).

on delicate woollen clothes Sponge immediately with a warm, fairly concentrated completely dissolved solution of mild detergent such as Dreft. Launder as usual. On dried stains use a liquid stain remover, such as Beaucaire, followed by laundering.

Coffee

on carpets Spoon and blot up as much as possible. Flush out the stain with a squirt from a soda syphon or sponge with warm water and blot dry. This will probably deal with fresh black coffee stains. For remaining marks and white coffee use a carpet shampoo or a carpet spotting kit eg Bissell. When dry, remove any final traces with a liquid stain remover, eg Dabitoff. Dried coffee stains may respond to repeated flushings with a soda syphon. Blot when effervescing stops and allow time to dry naturally between each application.

on non-washable fabrics and upholstery Treat as for COCOA on the same surfaces. Coffee stains on acrylic velvet, eg Dralon, should be thoroughly blotted with tissue or a cloth. Sprinkle any remaining stain with a warm solution of enzyme washing powder (15ml powder per 1 litre water) and rub lightly with a sponge in the direction of the pile. This avoids over-wetting. Flat-weave Dralons can be similarly treated. Old stains should be lubricated with a glycerine solution (equal parts glycerine and warm water), left for up to an hour then rinsed with a cloth wrung out in warm water. Blot well.

on table linen and washable fabrics Treat as for COCOA on the same surfaces.

Cosmetics *see* FOUNDATION CREAM; LIPSTICK; LOTIONS.

Crayon

on vinyl wallcoverings and bedheads A wipe with a damp cloth may be sufficient. If not, use a general purpose household cleaner, eg Handy Andy, or the stain remover Mangers De-Solv-it.

on painted walls Re-painting may be necessary and Polycell Stain Block can be used to obliterate marking and stains on painted surfaces to stop them reappearing when the surface is redecorated.

on wallpaper There is no treatment for this. Tear, not cut, another piece of wallpaper to cover the area and paste it over. On dense patterns this should give a fairly invisible mend, though it will tend to show on plain papers.

Cream (edible) *see* FATS, GREASE AND OILS.

Creosote

on non-washable fabrics Professional cleaning is advisable.

on washable fabrics Hold an absorbent pad on the right side and dab liquid lighter fuel or eucalyptus oil on the wrong side to push the stain out. Launder as usual. Old dried creosote stains are difficult to remove but may be softened sufficiently with glycerine solution (equal parts glycerine and warm water) left on for half an hour, to be washed out.

Curry

on carpets Scrape up any deposit and rub the stain lightly with a cloth wrung out of a solution of laundry borax (15ml borax to 500ml warm water). If this fails, rub a little neat glycerine into the carpet pile, or moisten with water and rub with Vanish stain removing bar. Leave for about ten minutes, then sponge out with warm water. Blot dry. This is a difficult stain and large marks should be cleaned professionally.

on non-washable fabrics Sponge with a warm laundry borax solution as for carpets; if this does not remove the stain have the item dry-cleaned professionally.

on table cloths and washable fabrics Rinse well in lukewarm water. Rub in glycerine solution (equal parts glycerine and warm water), leave for an hour and rinse again. Launder, using an enzyme detergent if suitable. Stubborn stains may be bleached out of fabrics other than nylon with a hydrogen peroxide solution (1 part 20 vol hydrogen peroxide to 6 parts cold water). Alternatively, try Stain Devils Ball Point Pen Stain Remover.

Cycle oil *see* CAR AND CYCLE OIL.

Dents

on wood see PART 3, FURNITURE, REMOVING MARKS.

Drinks *see* BEER; GIN AND OTHER SPIRITS; WINE.

Duplicating inks and toner

Gestetner duplicating ink

on clothes and upholstery Dab marks with a cotton-wool pad moistened with neat washing-up liquid. Sponge or launder where possible. The manufacturers produce a solvent called Klenzene for removing this ink from hands and clothes (*see* ADDRESSES).

Rank Xerox toner powder

(As used in this firm's duplicating machines.)

on washable fabrics and upholstery Brush, blow or vacuum to remove the powder deposit. Any light marking which remains can be washed out using a lukewarm solution of mild synthetic detergent. Hot water will set the stain.

on non-washable fabrics and upholstery Take these articles for professional cleaning; point out that the stain has been caused by a thermoplastic powder, as certain cleaning solvents will bond the powder to man-made fibres.

Dyes

on floors It is essential to wipe up splashes or spills immediately with a dry absorbent cloth. Avoid the use of water. There is no remedy for dried stains.

on non-washable fabrics, upholstery and carpets Carefully sponge with methylated spirit (not acetate or triacetate fibres) to which you have added a few drops of household ammonia. Alternatively and more safely, have the item dry-cleaned professionally.

on washable fabrics Soak white and fast-coloured fabrics in an enzyme detergent solution (not silk, wool, rubberized or flame-resistant fabrics) to clear discolouration caused by dyes. Launder. Alternatively, on white fabrics, use Stain Devils Colour Run Remover. Dylon Run Away colour run remover can also be used and is suitable for white and colourfast fabrics. The initial recommended tests should be carried out.

Egg

on carpets Scrape and use a dry cloth to remove as much of the deposit as possible. Treat with a liquid stain remover, eg Beaucaire, The Stain Slayer, followed, where necessary, by a carpet shampoo. Alternatively use a carpet spotting kit (*see* ADDRESSES).

on non-washable fabrics and upholstery Scrape off the surface deposit. Sponge egg white with cold salt water then clear water. Blot dry. Use K2R Stain Remover Spray if necessary. On egg yolk work in the lather from a washing-up detergent solution or upholstery shampoo. Wipe with a damp cloth. When dry, use a stain remover, eg Dabitoff aerosol, if necessary. For whole egg use a stain remover or upholstery spotting kit (*see* ADDRESSES).

on table linen and washable fabrics Sponge white of egg with cold salt water. Rinse. If the stain still shows when dry, soak and launder in an enzyme detergent solution if the fabric is suitable. Sponge whole egg with cold salt water then launder, using an enzyme detergent where suitable. Dried stains can usually be removed by soaking in an enzyme detergent solution (not silk, wool, rubberized or flame-resistant fabrics), followed by laundering. Launder yolk of egg using an enzyme detergent if possible. Apply an aerosol stain remover when dry to clear any traces.

Embroidery transfer

on fabrics This can usually be removed by touching lightly with methylated spirit (not on acetate or triacetate fabrics) applied on a cotton bud or cotton-wool wrapped round an orange stick. Test carefully first on the edge of the fabric. Launder if possible. Where methylated spirit cannot be used, laundering may be sufficient. Specialist cleaning should be considered for valuable items. The Royal School of Needlework will advise and give estimates (*see* ADDRESSES).

Face cream *see* FOUNDATION CREAM.

Fats, grease and oils

on carpets Blot up or scrape off deposit. Apply a stain remover, eg Kleeneze Carpet Spot Remover or The Stain Slayer. Take particular care where there is a foam or rubber-latexed backing. For heavy deposits apply Mangers De-Solv-it or use an iron and blotting paper as described in CANDLEWAX ON CARPETS. When no more grease can be removed, brush or rub in the lather from a solution of a dry foam carpet shampoo, eg Bissell. Traces of the deposit may continue to creep up (called 'wicking back' in the trade) for some time and you may need to repeat the application.

on leather shoes The maker's preparation of shoe leather, together with regular cleaning, usually gives a protective surface from which grease or cooking oil can be wiped without trace – if done quickly. Some fancy leathers may stain and the use of a rubber adhesive, as described below for upholstery and handbags, should deal with this. Alternatively use Meltonian Mel on stubborn marks and Meltonian Stain Remover on light ones. Clean both shoes completely to disguise any light patches.

on leather upholstery and handbags Cover the stain with a thin layer of bicycle puncture repair adhesive. A test area is essential since most adhesives contain colouring matter which could stain lighter shades. Leave for 24 hours then roll off carefully – it should have absorbed the grease. Treat the article with a good quality hide food, eg Connolly's Cee Bee Hide Food (except dyed leather without surface protection), Hidelife (not handbags).

on non-washable fabrics and upholstery Spread French chalk, talcum powder or powdered starch over a small mark. Replace

when it becomes impregnated with oil. Leave for several hours then brush clear. Alternatively, use a proprietary stain remover such as Beaucaire. An aerosol stain remover is advised for foam backed items. Grease on flat-woven and velvet-pile Dralon should be treated with Thawpit or Beaucaire. For larger areas (though not on Dralon or other pile fabrics) press with a warm iron over clean blotting paper to absorb the deposit and finally apply a stain remover, eg Beaucaire.

on suede coats Manufacturers of suede coats usually supply a cleaning pad or brush which will remove light stains. Failing this, use a suede cleaning cloth, eg Swade Groom, or a cleaning block such as Swade Aid. It is inadvisable to use a liquid cleaner as different types of grease and oil require different treatments and the use of chemicals can affect the dye irrevocably. Large, obvious stains require professional treatment.

on suede shoes Blot the stain with a tissue. Light stains should respond to a block suede cleaner such as Swade Aid. For heavier marking, and after a test on the instep, lightly wipe the stain with a cloth over a pad of cotton-wool which has been moistened with lighter fuel or Meltonian Mel. With the latter it is best to treat the whole shoe to avoid a patchy appearance.

on table linen Blot or scrape off any deposit. Cotton and linen can be laundered at sufficiently high temperatures to remove any marks. Other fabrics should be treated with a stain remover, eg The Stain Slayer, Stain Devils Grease & Oil Stain Remover before laundering.

on ties see PART 3, TIES

on wallpaper   Use a warm iron over clean blotting paper to draw out as much grease as possible. K2R Stain Remover Spray aerosol can be used to clear remaining marks. For hessian wallcovering use an aerosol stain remover, eg K2R Stain Remover Spray, very sparingly and check first for dye change as fairly weak colours are used in hessians.

on washable fabrics   Scrape off any deposit. Fabrics that can be laundered in hot water should come clean after this. On other fabrics use a stain remover first, eg Beaucaire, Stain Devils Grease & Oil Stain Remover. Heavy deposits, including car and cycle oil, should be rubbed with Swarfega Hand Cleanser or treated with Mangers De-Solv-it before laundering. Delicate fabrics and wool should be dabbed with eucalyptus oil then laundered or sponged.

Felt-tip stains *see* INK.

Fish oil *see* FATS, GREASE AND OILS.

Flower stains

on clothes   Laundering will usually remove these. Otherwise rub the marks with methylated spirit (not on acetate or triacetate fabrics) then sponge with warm water.

in vases and bowls   Fill them with water to which you have added a few drops of household bleach, eg Domestos, or denture cleaner, eg Steradent. Allow to soak for half an hour then rinse. Alternatively use a stain remover such as Chempro T.

Fly specks

on fabric lampshades   Try the careful use of an aerosol stain remover, eg K2R or Goddard's Dry Clean. If this fails, make up a warm solution of a heavy duty detergent, eg Persil, and brush over the stains from both sides using a soft brush (an old, soft toothbrush would be good). Rinse the area in the same way with clear water. Blot and allow to dry naturally away from direct heat in order to prevent ring marking or splitting. Do not wet the trimming; protect it with a towel.

on upholstery fabrics   Dab with a stain remover, eg Thawpit, or methylated spirit (not on acetate or triacetate materials). Test first. Alternatively try an aerosol stain remover, eg Goddard's Dry Clean.

on vellum and plastic lampshades   Wipe with a damp cloth wrung out in soapy water. Wipe with clear water and allow to dry.

Foundation cream

on upholstery and non-washable fabrics Wipe up any wet deposit carefully. Brush a dried stain with a soft brush to clear any powder. Apply a stain remover using an aerosol, eg K2R Stain Remover Spray, for fabrics which might ring mark with liquids. Alternatively, talcum powder or french chalk can be rubbed into light-coloured fabrics; after 2 hours shake and brush lightly with a soft-bristled brush. An upholstery spotting kit eg Bissell may also be used.

on washable fabrics Wipe a fresh stain to clear the surface deposit and, where possible, soak for 5 minutes in a weak ammonia solution (5ml ammonia to 500ml warm water). Rinse well. Launder at the highest temperature suited to the fabric. Dried stains should be brushed to remove the powder content, softened by lubricating with a glycerine solution (equal parts glycerine and warm water) left on up to an hour, before laundering. Stain Devils Make-up Stain Remover is also effective and should be used before laundering.

Fruit Juice

on carpets Act quickly. Scoop up and absorb as much as possible with paper towels. Rub the stain with Vanish stain removing bar and shampoo the area. When dry, remove any remaining traces by dabbing with a cloth moistened in methylated spirit. Stain Devils Fruit & Wine Stain Remover can also be used (except on latex and foam backed carpet) following a test on a hidden area.

on table linen Rinse under a cold tap then stretch the stained part of the fabric over a basin and pour hot water through it. Lubricate any remaining stain with a glycerine solution (equal parts glycerine and warm water), leave for half an hour and launder as usual. Dried stains may need to be covered with laundry borax powder before hot water is poured through. Alternatively use Stain Devils Fruit & Wine Stain Remover and rinse well.

on upholstery and non-washable fabrics Sponge with cold water and blot dry. Use an upholstery stain removal kit (*see* ADDRESSES) or a Spotkleen Stain Removing Cloth for small stains.

on washable fabrics Rinse under a cold tap. Clear remaining stain with Stain Devils Fruit & Wine Stain Remover. Alternatively, soak and launder with heavy duty detergent if the fabric is suitable. Dried stains should be lubricated with glycerine solution (equal parts glycerine and warm water) and left up to an hour before treating as suggested. Very stubborn stains on fabrics other than nylon may respond to careful bleaching with a hydrogen peroxide solution (1 part 20 vol peroxide to 6 parts cold water). White or coloured fabrics can be soaked in a germicidal fabric cleanser, eg Napisan, following the manufacturer's instructions.

Gin and other spirits

on carpets Blot up excess fluid and flush the mark with a squirt from a soda syphon or sponge with a cloth lightly wrung out in warm water. Blot well. If staining remains, apply the lather of a carpet shampoo, eg Bissell, or use a carpet spotting kit (*see* ADDRESSES). Sponging with methylated spirit may reduce old stains.

on non-washable fabrics and upholstery Sponge with clear luke-warm water then blot dry. If staining remains, apply the lather from an upholstery shampoo solution or washing-up detergent. Rub lightly then wipe clear with a cloth wrung out in warm water and blot dry. Alternatively, use an upholstery spotting kit (*see* ADDRESSES). In the case of fabrics which would water mark, these should be taken for professional cleaning.

on table cloths and washable fabrics Rinse with clear warm water then launder as usual.

on wood see PART 3, FURNITURE, REMOVING MARKS.

Grass stains

on cricket flannels Most 'flannels' are made of polyester so are washable. If washable, light staining should come out with laundering. For heavier marks, rub in Swarfega Hand Cleanser or dab with methylated spirit, then rinse in clear water before

laundering. True flannels are normally dry-cleaned and should be rubbed with a mixture of equal parts of cream of tartar powder and free-flow salt. Leave for 10 minutes then brush clear. Alternatively use a liquid stain remover, eg Beaucaire or the K2R Stain Remover Spray, repeating applications if necessary, or have the flannels dry-cleaned.

on washable clothes Light staining should wash out using a biological washing powder. With heavier marks, rub in Swarfega Hand Cleanser, dab with methylated spirit (not on acetate and triacetate materials) or use Stain Devils Fruit & Wine Stain Remover then rinse in clear water before laundering.

Gravy

on carpets Scoop up excess and wipe with a dry cloth to remove as much as possible. Treat with a liquid stain remover such as Beaucaire, or an aerosol or foam on latex-backed carpets followed by a carpet shampoo. Alternatively, use a carpet spotting kit (*see* ADDRESSES). Blot frequently to avoid over-wetting.

on non-washable fabrics Treat with an aerosol stain remover, eg Boots Dry Cleaner Spray Stain Remover.

on table linen and washable fabrics Soak in cool water then launder in warm detergent suds. Treat any grease marks remaining when dry with a liquid stain remover, eg Dabitoff. Dried stains should be soaked in an enzyme soak powder eg Bio-tex or an enzyme detergent solution (not silk, wool, rubberized or flame-resistant fabrics) before laundering.

Hair oil

on fabrics-upholstered headboards Treat with a stain remover, eg Thawpit or Dabitoff (both specially recommended for Dralons), or Goddard's Dry Clean. Do not over-apply, particularly on padded areas. Avoid marks recurring by having the headboard treated with a protective spray, eg Scotchgard (*see* ADDRESSES).

on wooden headboards Rub with a cloth moistened in white spirit. Buff well with a soft dry cloth.

on hessian wallcoverings Treat as for FATS, GREASE AND OILS on hessian wallcoverings.

on painted walls Wipe the stained area gently with a general purpose household cleaner used neat. Dab with a cloth wrung out in clean water.

on wallpaper Treat as for FATS, GREASE AND OILS on wallpaper.

on washable wallpaper Sponge the mark with a warm, well

diluted washing-up liquid solution. Rinse with a cloth wrung out in clear water and pat dry.

on vinyl Wipe gently with a cloth wrung out in a solution of general purpose household cleaner and rinse. Stubborn marks should be rubbed lightly with white spirit.

Hair spray

on mirrors Wipe with a cloth moistened in methylated spirit.

Heat marks

on wood see PART 3, FURNITURE, REMOVING MARKS.

Henna hair preparations

on skin Rub gently with the inside of the skin of a squeezed lemon and rinse well. Residual staining is likely to last for a couple of days.

on towels and washable fabrics Stains from henna shampoos and powder mixtures should be soaked in a biological pre-wash preparation eg Bio-tex or biological detergent where possible, then laundered with the latter or other heavy duty detergent. Marks should fade over several treatments but it may not be possible to clear the considerably more resistant powder staining. Treat henna wax preparations with a grease solvent eg The Stain Slayer prior to laundering. Bleaching is not advised for henna stains. Delicate and expensive articles should be dry cleaned.

on carpets and upholstery Since henna is a vegetable dye and particularly resistant, no home treatment is recommended and professional cleaning may not be successful in this instance. NB. Prevention is better than cure. Protect clothing and surroundings, and cover floor areas with a polythene sheet before starting a henna session.

Ice cream

on carpets Scrape up the deposit and wipe with a damp cloth to remove as much of the staining as possible. Apply a carpet shampoo. Alternatively use a carpet spotting kit (*see* ADDRESSES). Any grease marks which remain after the carpet has dried should be treated with a stain remover, eg Beaucaire (not on foam backed carpets), or K2R Stain Remover Spray.

on non-washable fabrics and upholstery Wipe off surface deposit. Sponge with lukewarm water. When dry treat any stain with a stain remover, eg Goddard's Dry Clean or K2R Stain Remover Spray aerosols. Remaining traces can be bleached out carefully with a hydrogen peroxide solution (1 part 20 vol peroxide to 6 parts cold water) if the fabric is suitable (not on nylon).

on washable fabrics Wipe off excess and soak in warm detergent suds. Use an enzyme detergent if the fabric is suitable. Launder in water as hot as the fabric can take. On fabrics that cannot be soaked, such as silk and wool, and also on other fabrics where the stain has dried, sponge with a warm laundry borax solution (15ml borax to 500ml water) or use Stain Devils Fruit & Wine Stain Remover before laundering. When dry, treat any grease marks with a stain remover, such as Beaucaire.

Ink

on wood see PART 3, FURNITURE, REMOVING MARKS.

Ballpoint ink

on fabrics and upholstery Act quickly or the stain may become impossible to remove. Remove as much as possible by pressing with pads of cotton wool or paper towels. Most types respond to light dabbing with methylated spirit applied on a cotton-wool bud (not on acetate or triacetate fabrics), or use Stain Devils Ball Point Pen Stain Remover. If a test section proves unsuccessful, contact the pen manufacturer for advice. Launder, if possible, after treatment. Obtain professional treatment for delicate fabrics such as jacket linings; intensive staining will also need professional help. The Association of British Laundry, Cleaning & Rental Services Ltd can advise (*see* ADDRESSES).

on suede handbags Try rubbing lightly with a fine emery cloth or the suede cleaning block Swade Aid. Failing this seek professional advice. It may not be possible to remove this stain.

on vinyl upholstery, wallcoverings, dolls and handbags Unless treated immediately this stain cannot be removed as the ink quickly merges into the plasticizer and causes permanent marking. Treat by scrubbing at once with a nail brush, using warm water and soap or detergent.

Felt-tip ink

on fabrics and upholstery Act quickly. Remove as much ink as possible by pressing with pads of cotton wool or paper towels. Small marks should be dabbed with methylated spirit (never use on acetate or triacetate materials). Where possible launder using soap powder or flakes. Alternatively, and for larger stains, use repeated applications of the aerosol stain remover K2R, or Stain Devils Felt Tip Pen Stain Remover.

on vinyl bedheads, wallcoverings, dolls and handbags Carefully use a household cleaner, eg Handy Andy, or methylated spirit. If these fail use neat washing-up liquid applied on a cloth over one finger. If all else fails, rub lightly with emery paper folded over a ruler edge. Finish with a car fabric and vinyl cleaner, eg Turtle Wax Upholstery Cleaner. It is worth contacting individual manufacturers for advice about heavy staining from their pens. Professional cleaning is advised for delicate fabrics and extensive staining.

Fountain-pen ink (washable)

on carpets Flush with a squirt from a soda syphon then blot with absorbent paper. Remove as much more ink as possible by applying cold water, blotting frequently to absorb the ink and to avoid over-wetting. Apply a hot soapflake solution to the stain leaving the pad in contact for 15 minutes. Repeat as necessary, blotting well between applications. Rinse by applying clean water. Blot well. Any small stains remaining on light-coloured carpets can be treated with a solution of sodium hydrosulphite (obtainable in powder form from certain chemists), using 25ml sodium hydrosulphite to 600ml water. Do a test first as it has a bleaching action. If satisfactory, apply small amounts, blotting between each. Rinse with warm water. Alternatively, after initial blotting, use a proprietary stain remover such as Shaws No-Stain Aerosol Spray or a carpet spotting kit. Old stains usually require professional treatment, though if you know the type of ink spilt, the manufacturer may be able to suggest a process (*see* ADDRESSES for Parker Pen inks).

on fabrics and upholstery Act quickly to prevent the stain drying. Sponge fabrics with, or rub under, cold water until no more ink can be removed. Launder if possible to clear traces. If marks remain after laundering, squeeze lemon juice over them and press the stained area between two pieces of white cotton cloth. Repeat as necessary, then rinse. Treat fresh stains on upholstery with an upholstery spotting kit (*see* ADDRESSES). Where this is not available, sponge gently with cold water and blot well to remove as much as possible. When dry, follow with repeated applications of a stain remover, eg K2R Stain Remover Spray to clear any traces.

Dried stains on white fabrics should respond to a weak solution of household bleach (though not on silk, wool, crease-resistant or drip-dry fabrics). Alternatively, dried stains on washable whites and coloureds can be treated with Stain Devils Mould & Ink Stain Remover. Try repeated applications of K2R aerosol on non-washable fabrics. Stains on delicate fabrics, expensive articles and upholstery should be treated professionally.

Iodine

on carpets Using a cotton-wool pad, carefully dab with a solution of photographic hypo (2.5ml to 250ml warm water). This is obtainable from chemists stocking photographic materials. As soon as the stain has been cleared, treat the area with a warm carpet shampoo solution. Blot to avoid over-wetting.

on non-washable fabrics and upholstery Professional dry-cleaning is recommended.

on washable fabrics and bedding Immediate laundering in rich soap suds with a few drops of ammonia added usually clears the stain. Soak stubborn and old stains briefly in a solution of photographic hypo (2.5ml to 250ml warm water). This is obtainable from chemists stocking photographic materials. Alternatively use Stain Devils Coffee & Tea Stain Remover. Rinse well and launder in the usual way.

Iron mould (rust marking)

on table linen and handkerchiefs Rub with lemon juice, cover the stain with salt and leave for up to an hour. Rinse and launder. If stains persist use a proprietary rust remover, eg Movol (white fabrics only), or Stain Devils Rust & Iron Mould Stain Remover (which can also be used on colourfast fabrics) and rinse well with the fabric held horizontally under a lukewarm running tap.

Jam, marmalade

on carpets Scoop up and wipe off any surface deposit with a cloth wrung out in warm water. Treat the area with a carpet shampoo. Alternatively use a carpet spotting kit eg Bissell. Any fruit colour remaining should respond to dabbing with methylated spirit.

on non-washable fabrics and upholstery Wipe off any surface deposit. Sponge the stain with a cloth moistened in a warm solution of washing-up liquid. If marks persist, rub a little laundry borax powder on the damp fabric, leave for ten minutes, then sponge clear. Blot well. Alternatively sponge the stain with clear warm water, allow to dry and apply K2R Stain Remover Spray or an upholstery spotting kit (*see* ADDRESSES).

on table linen and washable fabrics   Fresh stains can usually be washed out. Old stains should first be soaked in a laundry borax solution (15ml borax to 500ml warm water) for half an hour followed by laundering. Alternatively, use Stain Devils Fruit & Wine Stain Remover.

Ketchup and bottled sauces

on carpets   Scoop and wipe up excess with a clean damp cloth, being careful not to spread the stain. Dried stains can sometimes be softened by rubbing in a 50/50 solution of glycerine and water and leaving for half an hour. Sponge with clean warm water, blotting to avoid over-wetting. Gently rub lather from a whisked-up solution of carpet shampoo on to any remaining stain. Alternatively, use 1001 Troubleshooter. Wipe in the direction of the pile with a cloth wrung out in lukewarm water. When dry, repeated applications of an aerosol stain remover, eg K2R Stain Remover Spray should clear any traces.

on upholstery and non-washable fabrics   Scrape carefully with the back of a knife to remove excess. Wipe lightly with a clean damp cloth. Apply an aerosol stain remover, eg K2R Stain Remover Spray, when the fabric has dried. Professional treatment is advised for tomato-based sauces and delicate fabrics.

on washable fabrics   Immediate action is essential. Gather up the stained area and rinse under a cold tap. Use a pre-wash laundry aid eg Frend, Shout or Vanish, or loosen the stain by rubbing in equal parts of glycerine and warm water, then launder in heavy duty detergent. Stains should also respond to the use of Stain Devils Ball Point Pen Stain Remover.

Lipstick

on carpets   Scrape carefully with a blunt knife to remove any surface deposit, then treat with a stain remover such as Stain Devils Make-up Stain Remover or a carpet spotting kit eg Bissell. Clear indelible lipstick colour by careful application of methylated spirit on a cotton wool bud.

on gloss or emulsion-painted walls and vinyl wallcoverings   Rub the marks lightly with a damp cloth or one wrung out in a warm detergent solution. Stubborn marks may respond to a cream-type household cleaner such as Jif applied on a damp sponge.

on non-washable fabrics and upholstery   Use an aerosol stain remover such as Boots Dry Cleaner Spray Stain Remover or the liquid Stain Devils Make-up Stain Remover.

on table linen, towels and other washable fabrics Most stains will wash out although some types of lipstick may need an initial application of a suitable liquid stain remover, eg Stain Devils Make-up Stain Remover.

on wallpaper K2R Stain Remover Spray aerosol can be used on this. Stubborn marks and indelible lipstick may need to be covered by a new piece of wallpaper. If torn rather than cut to shape it will be less obvious when stuck on the wall.

Lotions

If greasy treat as under FATS, GREASE AND OILS. If non-greasy treat as under GIN AND OTHER SPIRITS.

Marmalade *see* JAM.

Mascara

on towels, clothes and upholstery Apply an aerosol stain remover such as Goddard's Dry Clean or liquid stain remover such as Stain Devils Make-up Stain Remover. If a stain still remains, dab with diluted ammonia (1 part ammonia to 3 parts cold water) but test coloureds as ammonia can cause dyes to run. Rinse the area thoroughly. Launder where possible.

... and thank you for providing such a very agreeable lady curate!

Mayonnaise

on non-washable fabrics Remove the residue with a damp cloth, taking care not to spread the stain. Treat the dry fabric with an aerosol stain remover such as K2R Stain Remover Spray. Professional cleaning is advisable for expensive garments. Alternatively, use Stain Devils Grease & Oil Stain Remover.

on table linen and washable fabrics Sponge with warm water (not hot which would set the egg content). Use an enzyme detergent to soak where possible, then launder in rich suds.

Medicines

Sponging with warm water followed by laundering, where possible, should remove most medicines, though methylated spirit may be necessary to take out final colour traces. It is sensible to consult a chemist as to what is in a particular medicine before attempting treatment. Have non-washable items professionally treated.

Metal polish

on carpets Spoon and blot up as much as possible. Dab the area with white spirit. Use a stiff carpet brush to clear the powdery deposit when the pile has dried. Shampoo if necessary. Dried stains should be brushed before treatment is applied.

on fabrics Wipe with a tissue to clear as much of the deposit as possible. Apply a stain remover such as Boots Dry Cleaner. Laundering should remove traces from washable fabrics.

on non-washable fabrics Sponge off as much as possible and brush well when dry. Treat any remaining marks with an aerosol stain remover eg K2R Stain Remover Spray.

Mildew

on leather, shoes and cases Sponge the leather with a mild disinfectant solution, eg pine (5ml disinfectant to 500ml warm water). Alternatively, wipe over with a cotton-wool pad moistened with an antiseptic mouth wash, used neat. Wipe and buff dry with a soft cloth. Follow with an application of a good quality hide food, eg Connolly's Cee Bee Hide Food (except on dyed leather with no surface protection), or shoe polish in the case of shoes.

on non-washable fabrics and upholstery Brushing out of doors will clear some of the spores. Spray with Mystox solution to kill the rest (*see* ADDRESSES). The smell should disappear after 3 or 4 days. Dry cleaning may clear remaining marks although the careful use of 20 vol. hydrogen peroxide, where possible, is likely to be more successful (1 part 20 vol peroxide to 6 parts cold water). Rinse. For articles of value it is sensible to consult a museum such as the Victoria and Albert (*see* ADDRESSES).

on plastic shower curtains Sponge with a weak solution of household bleach or antiseptic to clear light marking. Areas heavily stained with this minute fungus-like growth can be swabbed with a mild detergent solution then treated with a solution of a proprietary bactericide, eg Fungo (*see* ADDRESSES).

on wall surfaces Wash down the wall with a mild detergent solution. Follow by wiping over with a solution of a proprietary bactericide, eg Fungo (*see* ADDRESSES).

on washable fabrics Laundering usually removes mildew marking while the growth is still fresh enough to be on the surface. Traces which remain on white fabrics (except nylon) can be treated by bleaching with a hydrogen peroxide solution (1 part 20 vol peroxide to 6 parts cold water). A solution of household bleach should be used on white cottons or linens (though not on crease-resistant, drip-dry, embossed or piqué fabrics). On coloureds, rub the dampened areas with hard soap and dry in the sun. Regular washing will reduce marks. Stain Devils Mould & Ink Stain Remover can be used on white and colourfast fabrics (not acetates).

Milk

on carpets Speedy treatment is vital to stop penetration and drying, otherwise the smell is virtually impossible to eradicate. Use a soda syphon or lukewarm water to flush the area well and blot thoroughly. Next use a carpet spot stain remover, eg 1001 Troubleshooter or a carpet spotting kit eg Bissell. Although it may be possible to remove dried stains yourself, professional cleaning may still be necessary to clear the smell which becomes apparent whenever the room warms up. However, it would be worth trying CP-60 aerosol cleaner which has effective deodorising properties.

on non-washable fabrics and upholstery Sponge with lukewarm water. Blot well. If a stain remains when the fabric is dry, use a stain remover, eg Goddard's Dry Clean aerosol, Thawpit (recommended for use on Dralons). Alternatively, use an upholstery spotting kit eg Bissell.

on table linen and washable fabrics Rinse well in lukewarm water then launder in warm detergent suds. When dry, treat any remaining mark with a stain remover, eg Beaucaire. Dried stains can be soaked before laundering in an enzyme detergent solution, if the fabric is suitable, otherwise, with the exception of nylon, in a hydrogen peroxide solution (1 part 20 vol hydrogen peroxide to 6 parts cold water).

Mud

on carpets Allow the mud to dry completely, then brush off with a stiff-bristled carpet brush and vacuum. Use a carpet spot cleaner, eg 1001 Troubleshooter, Kleeneze Carpet Spot Cleaner or a carpet spotting kit eg Bissell. Any colour traces that remain should be dabbed lightly with methylated spirit.

on non-washable fabrics and upholstery Allow the mud to dry completely then lightly brush off. Sponge remaining marks with a warm, mild detergent solution. Wipe with a cloth wrung out in clear water and blot well. On coats (not waterproof) and heavy clothing, use a stain remover such as Goddard's Dry Clean on marks remaining after the initial brushing.

on washable fabrics Laundering should remove mud staining but use a soft brush on dried deposits and treat heavy marking with a proprietary stain remover before washing as usual.

Mustard
Ready-mixed English mustard

on non-washable fabrics Where a fabric will not ring mark, sponge with a solution of mild synthetic detergent and remove any remaining colour by sponging with an ammonia solution (5ml ammonia to 500ml water). Blot with a towel to avoid over-wetting and finish with clear water. Delicate fabrics and those likely to ring mark should be treated professionally. It is important to tell the cleaner which type of mustard is involved.

on table linen and washable fabrics Rub the stained area in a warm solution of mild synthetic detergent, eg Dreft, then remove any remaining stain by sponging with an ammonia solution (5ml ammonia to 500ml water). Launder.

Powdered (made-up) mustard

For prepared varieties of American, French and German mustard, follow the same procedure.

on non-washable fabrics Professional dry-cleaning is recommended. Tell the cleaner which type of mustard is involved.

on washable fabrics Laundering should clear the stain. Lubricate dried stains with a glycerine solution (equal parts glycerine and warm water) and leave for up to an hour before laundering. Stubborn stains should respond to Stain Devils Ball Point Pen Stain Remover.

Nail varnish

on carpets Scoop and carefully wipe up as much of the deposit as possible with paper tissues, trying to avoid spreading the stain. Dab the mark with a pad of cotton-wool moistened with amyl acetate, after testing near the edge of the carpet. A pad with non-oily nail varnish remover can also be used following an initial test. Over-soaking with these solvents could damage carpet backings. Alternatively use a carpet spotting kit eg Bissell. Any remaining colour should respond to dabbing with methylated spirit. Finish by applying a foam carpet shampoo eg 1001 Troubleshooter or the lather of a carpet shampoo solution eg Bissell, to the treated area.

on fabrics and upholstery Wipe up spills immediately, using absorbent paper or cotton-wool. Where possible, hold a white absorbent pad beneath the stain and dab with amyl acetate (safe on most fabrics but a test area is advised). A pad with non-oily nail varnish remover can also be used, but not on acetates and triacetates. Any colouring remaining can usually be cleared by dabbing with methylated spirit but this should never be used on acetate or triacetate. Launder the fabric where possible. Stain Devils Tar & Paint Stain Remover should clear this stain. Heavy spills on acetate and triacetate need professional cleaning.

Nicotine *see* TOBACCO STAINS.

Oil *see* CAR AND CYCLE OIL; FATS, GREASE AND OILS; HAIR OIL; PARAFFIN OIL.

Orange juice *see* FRUIT JUICE.

Paints

GENERAL NOTE
More recently-developed types of paint, where cleaning the brushes in a washing-up liquid solution is recommended in the instructions, can usually be removed from most surfaces by laundering or sponging immediately (don't wait until you've finished the painting job). It is essential in fact to treat all paint spills speedily as dried paint marks of any kind are very difficult to remove. With all paint spills, first scrape and wipe off as much as possible and then treat according to type. (*See also* ARTISTS' PAINTS.)

Emulsion and water-based undercoat
Treat wet paint by sponging immediately with cold water, taking care to mop carefully round the edges to avoid spreading the stain. Launder in warm suds where possible. Stains not more than 5 hours old may respond to Stain Devils Tar & Paint Stain Remover. Dried emulsion stains are difficult to remove. Try using methylated spirit to soften the deposit but take care that it does not affect any colour (do not use an acetate or triacetate fabrics). Follow by laundering or sponging. Delicate fabrics and large areas of dried emulsion on upholstery, carpets or clothing are best treated professionally – avoid home efforts.

Gloss (oil-based) and oil-based undercoat
Dab carefully with white spirit or use Mangers De-Solv-it or Stain Devils Tar & Paint Stain Remover after an initial test. Sponge with cold water and repeat the treatment if necessary. Launder where possible; shampoo carpets and upholstery. Alternatively use a

carpet or upholstery spotting kit (*see* ADDRESSES). Treat dried stains with Mangers De-Solv-it after an initial test. Work it into the stain with the fingers. Dried paint takes longer to break down so you'll require patience. Bad marks and acetate and viscose fabrics need professional treatment.

Paraffin oil

on carpets Do not smoke as paraffin is highly flammable. Tackle the mark at once as oil which penetrates to the back of a carpet can cause dye seepage and deterioration of foam or rubber-latexed backing. Mop up as much as possible with absorbent paper or rags then use an aerosol stain remover, such as Goddard's Dry Clean or Mangers De-Solv-it, repeating applications until the mark clears. Large areas of stain should be cleaned professionally.

on non-washable fabrics Treat as FATS, GREASE AND OILS on non-washable fabrics.

on washable fabrics Treat as FATS, GREASE AND OILS on washable fabrics.

Perfume

on non-washable fabrics Lubricate with a glycerine solution (equal parts glycerine and warm water), leave for up to an hour then wipe carefully with a cloth wrung out in warm water, taking care not to over-wet the fabric. Blot dry. Expensive clothes, particularly silk, should be cleaned professionally.

on washable fabrics Rinse immediately. If the stain has dried, lubricate with a glycerine solution (equal parts glycerine and warm water) and leave for up to an hour, or use Vanish before laundering as usual.

Perspiration

on non-washable fabrics Dab with a solution of white vinegar (15ml vinegar to 250ml warm water) which should help both to clear the stain and deodorize the area. Where dye has been affected, light rubbing with methylated spirit may help. Neither should be used on acetate or triacetate and they could damage some viscose fabrics. Men's suits are often lined with these fabrics and should be cleaned professionally, as should any garments that are heavily stained.

on washable fabrics Sponge fresh stains with a weak solution of ammonia (5ml ammonia to 500ml warm water) and rinse immediately. Where colour has been affected sponge with a white vinegar solution (15ml vinegar to 250ml warm water) and rinse. Suitable fabrics can be soaked in an enzyme detergent solution. Alternatively, white fabrics other than nylon can usually be bleached with a hydrogen peroxide solution (1 part 20 vol peroxide to 6 parts cold water) or treated with Stain Devils Coffee & Tea Stain Remover. Finally, launder as usual, adding a little vinegar to the rinse water.

Photo-copier toner *see* DUPLICATING INKS

Pitch *see* TAR.

Plasticine

on jerseys, worsted trousers, carpets and upholstery Carefully scrape off as much as possible. Hold an absorbent pad under the stain, if possible, and dab it with a liquid stain remover, eg Thawpit, Beaucaire, to dissolve the deposit. On small areas, dabbing with liquid lighter fuel may do the trick but this needs care on synthetic fabrics. Avoid dampening the carpet backing. Washable fabrics should then be laundered as usual, non-washables sponged gently with warm water and blotted dry at once.

Rain spots

on calf leather coats, handbags, shoes Before the spots dry, wipe with a clean cloth then allow to dry naturally. Leather Groom is a foam cleaner, polisher and conditioner suited to all coloured leather. It leaves a water-repellant surface.
on suede clothes Allow rain spots to dry naturally, then use the manufacturer's special suede cleaning pad, a soft bristled brush or a suede cleaning cloth such as Swade Groom.
on suede shoes Treat as for suede clothes. *See also* PART 3, LEATHER.

Raspberry *see* FRUIT JUICE.

Resins *see* CREOSOTE; SHELLAC.

Ribena *see* FRUIT JUICE.

Rubber

perished from hot-water bottles on sheets; hot-water bottle covers Hold an absorbent pad below the mark and rub with liquid lighter fuel. Launder as usual.

Rum *see* GIN AND OTHER SPIRITS.

Rust marks

on bath see BATH STAINS.

on carpets Use a proprietary rust remover, eg Stain Devils Rust & Iron Mould Stain Remover (*see* ADDRESSES), following the maker's instructions.

on non-washable fabrics Use a proprietary rust remover, eg Stain Devils Rust & Iron Mould Stain Remover (*see* ADDRESSES), following the maker's instructions.

on washable fabrics Rub marks with neat lemon juice then rinse. Alternatively use a proprietary rust remover, such as Movol (white fabrics only) or Stain Devils Rust & Iron Mould Stain Remover. Launder as usual.

Salad dressing *see* FATS, GREASE AND OILS, or MAYONNAISE, according to type.

Salt and water marking

on calf leather boots Re-dampen the mark with a sponge or cloth, then dry off by rubbing with a soft absorbent cloth. Failing this, use Punch Salt Stain Remover or Meltonian Stain Remover on the stain and then lightly over the whole boot or shoe to counteract any colour change.

on suede shoes Allow the suede to dry out naturally then use a proprietary stain remover, eg Punch Salt Stain Remover or Meltonian Stain Remover, using a suede brush to raise the nap when dry.

Scent *see* PERFUME.

Scorch marks

on carpets Where scorching is slight it may be possible to trim the tufts with scissors. Otherwise use a stiff-bristled brush to remove any loosened fibres. Then take a wire brush or piece of coarse glasspaper and make gentle circular movements to hide the area. Some carpet retailers are prepared to re-tuft or patch damaged areas but this is an expensive job to have done.

on non-washable fabrics Use a glycerine solution (equal parts glycerine and warm water) to lubricate light marks, leave up to an hour then sponge with warm water. On heavier marks, sponge with a cloth wrung out in a laundry borax solution (15ml borax t

500ml warm water). Rinse and repeat treatment if necessary, taking care not to over-wet.

on washable fabrics Light marks should be rubbed, fabric to fabric, under cold running water, then soaked in a warm laundry borax solution (15ml borax to 500ml warm water) until clear. Rinse and launder as usual. Heavy marks cannot usually be removed completely, although those on white fabrics, except nylon, will sometimes respond to careful bleaching with a hydrogen peroxide solution (1 part 20 vol peroxide to 6 parts cold water).

Scratches

on wood see PART 3, FURNITURE, REMOVING MARKS.

Sea water marks *see* SALT AND WATER MARKING.

Shellac

on non-washable fabrics Act quickly before it has a chance to dry and harden. Dab lightly with a cotton-wool pad moistened with methylated spirit (not on acetate or triacetate fabrics). Follow by wiping with a cloth wrung out of a warm synthetic detergent solution. Finish with clear water and blot well. Professional treatment will be necessary for delicate fabrics and dried stains.

on washable fabrics Act immediately, dabbing the stain with

methylated spirit (not on acetate or triacetate fabrics). Once shellac has dried, it may be possible to soften it sufficiently with methylated spirit so that any remaining deposit and colour can be laundered or sponged out with a synthetic detergent solution.

Shoe polish

on carpets Scrape off as much of the deposit as possible. Dab either with a stain remover or white spirit to dissolve any remaining particles. If any stain remains, dab with methylated spirit and finally shampoo the treated area. Alternatively treat the mark with a carpet spotting kit (*see* ADDRESSES) after scraping off the deposit.
on non-washable fabrics Scrape off as much of the deposit as possible. Treat as for carpets (above) and finish off by sponging with warm water then blotting dry.
on fabrics Either use a stain remover, eg K2R Stain Remover Spray, to remove the mark, or use a few drops of ammonia in the water when laundering. Heavy marking will need treatment with a liquid stain remover such as Mangers De-Solv-it or white spirit before rinsing and laundering.

Smoke and soot

on brickwork Use a soft brush or vacuum cleaner attachment to remove soot, then scrub with a hard scrubbing brush and clear warm water. If soiling does not respond, try wiping down with malt vinegar (this may also remove burn marks), followed by thorough rinsing. Heavy soot staining may need to be treated with a solution of spirits of salts (1 part spirits of salts to 6 parts water), but do not allow it to come into contact with the cement between the bricks. Wash down quickly and thoroughly with plenty of warm water. **Spirits of salts is corrosive**, so wear gloves and goggles and protect clothing; it also gives off extremely strong and **poisonous fumes**, so see that the room is well ventilated and do not lean over the surface while applying the solution.
on carpets Do not brush as this might spread the mark. Vacuum the area or shake the carpet or rug gently, out of doors if possible. Small marks will usually come out with an aerosol stain remover, such as K2R Stain Remover Spray. Large areas of stain are best cleaned professionally, though they may respond to light brushing with the lather of a carpet shampoo solution. On light-coloured carpets, use repeated applications of French chalk or Fuller's Earth. Rub in lightly and vacuum off when the powder has absorbed the soot.

on stonework Follow fireplace manufacturer's cleaning instructions when available. Otherwise scrub with clear water. Use a mild solution of washing-up liquid on light marks and a concentrated solution of domestic bleach on heavy marks. Rinse thoroughly.

Soft drinks *see* FRUIT JUICE.

Soup

on carpets Scoop up spillage. Immediately use a foam carpet cleaner eg Bissell 'Not on the Carpet' Accident Cleaner to clear the stain and smell.

on non-washable fabrics Scoop and blot spillage. Wipe the area with a warm damp sponge and allow to dry. After testing on a hidden area, apply a spray stain remover such as Boots Dry Clean Spray Stain Remover.

on washable fabrics Rinse the stained area with warm water. Soak and launder using biological detergent where possible.

Spirits *see* GIN AND OTHER SPIRITS.

Sweat *see* PERSPIRATION.

Syrup *see* JAM.

Tar

on carpets Scrape gently to remove the deposit. Very hard marks may be given an initial softening with a glycerine solution (equal parts glycerine and warm water). Leave for up to an hour then rinse with clear water and blot well. Use either a carpet spotting kit (*see* ADDRESSES) or, when dry, a stain remover, eg The Stain Slayer, Dabitoff. Obstinate stains will sometimes respond to dabbing with eucalyptus oil or Swarfega Hand Cleanser, lightly rubbed into the pile. Rinse with sparing applications of cold water, blotting with a towel to prevent over-wetting.

on non-washable fabrics Treat as tar on carpets, above.

on leather shoes After an initial test on the instep, try dabbing with liquid lighter fuel or use Meltonian Mel.

on suede shoes Following a successful test, try a very careful application of Meltonian Mel. If the test is unsuccessful, get professional advice from a good shoe shop.

on swimwear, beach towels and other washable fabrics Scrape carefully to remove as much surface deposit as possible. Hold an absorbent pad over the stain and dab it from below with cotton-wool moistened with eucalyptus oil. Alternatively, on non-rubberized items you can use a stain remover, such as The Stain Slayer, Dabitoff or Swarfega Hand Cleanser rubbed into the stain. Launder.

Tea

on blankets Rinse at once in warm water. If the mark has dried, try bleaching it carefully with hydrogen peroxide solution (1 part 20 vol peroxide to 6 parts cold water). Rinse and launder. On Acrilan blankets laundering may suffice. Alternatively, use Stain Devils Coffee & Tea Stain Remover.

on carpets Blot thoroughly. If the spill is recent, flush the area with a squirt from a soda syphon or sponge with warm water. When necessary, and where the tea contained milk, use a carpet shampoo eg Sabco, Kleeneze. When dry, apply an aerosol stain remover such as K2R if any traces remain. Dried tea stains should first be sponged with laundry borax solution (15ml borax to 500ml warm water). If marking remains, rub in a glycerine solution (equal parts glycerine and warm water), leave for up to an hour then rinse with clear water and use a carpet shampoo, following the manufacturer's instructions.

on non-washable fabrics and upholstery Sponge with a laundry borax solution (15ml borax to 500ml warm water) then with clear water. Blot well. When dry, use an aerosol stain remover, eg Goddard's Dry Clean on any remaining traces. Alternatively, use an upholstery spotting kit (*see* ADDRESSES).

on table linen Rinse immediately under a cold tap. Clear traces by soaking and laundering, preferably in enzyme detergent solution, provided the fabric is suitable. Dried tea stains should be dampened, stretched over a basin, sprinkled with laundry borax powder and hot water poured through prior to laundering. Alternatively, use Stain Devils StainSalts to boost the washing detergent during the laundering process.

on washable fabrics Rinse fresh stains in lukewarm water then launder, using an enzyme detergent if the fabric is suitable. Use a pre-wash laundry aid eg Frend to loosen dried stains prior to laundering. Alternatively remove them with Stain Devils Coffee & Tea Stain Remover.

Tide marks *see* BATH STAINS.

Tipp-Ex fluid

on carpets and upholstery Allow to dry and pick off as much residue as possible. Professional cleaning is required to clear the remainder.

on clothes and other fabrics Although the stain may come out of washable items after several washes, professional cleaning is recommended for these and 'dry clean only' articles.

Tobacco

on hands Rub neat Milton 2 Sterilizing Fluid on to the stained areas with a pad of cotton-wool. Wash your hands in the usual way.

Tomato juice *see* FRUIT JUICE.

Ketchup see KETCHUP AND BOTTLED SAUCES.

Purée see KETCHUP AND BOTTLED SAUCES.

Treacle *see* JAM.

Urine

on carpets   Treat as soon as possible with Bissell 'Not on the Carpet' Accident Cleaner which will also deodorise. Alternatively, flush the area with a squirt from a soda syphon or sponge with cold water and blot well. Sponge the damp area with carpet shampoo solution. Rinse several times with cold water with a few drops of antiseptic added. Blot well each time. Where a dried stain has affected the dye, sponge with an ammonia solution (2.5ml ammonia to 500ml cold water). Blot thoroughly. CP-60 aerosol cleaner also removes any unpleasant after-smell.

on leather shoes   Provided the urine is wiped off at once with a cloth lightly wrung out in warm water, no staining should remain. Buff gently. Where urine is allowed to dry out, rubbing with a damp cloth will achieve only superficial removal of the salts which have penetrated the leather. In this case, the treatment should be repeated from time to time as the perspiration from the foot gradually drives the salts to the surface. The marks should respond to Punch Salt Stain Remover.

on mattresses   This is more easily done by two people as the mattress is best turned on its side and held in position while treatment is carried out. Press a towel below the stained area and sponge with a cold solution of washing-up liquid or upholstery shampoo. Wipe with cold water to which you have added a few drops of antiseptic, eg Dettol, Milton. Alternatively use Bissell 'Not on the Carpet' Accident Cleaner aerosol or an upholstery spotting kit eg Bissell. It is probable that a ring mark will remain, but full treatment is nonetheless necessary both to remove the urine (which could cause the fabric to rot) and deodorize the area.

on non-washable fabrics   Fresh stains should be sponged with cold water. Blot well. Sponge remaining stain with a vinegar solution (15ml vinegar to 500ml warm water). Dried stains require professional cleaning.

on suede shoes   Penetration is rapid, so act quickly. Rub the marks lightly with a cloth well wrung out in warm water. Raise the suede nap by brushing while still damp with a suede brush. Dried marks may be difficult to remove but it is worth trying a suede and leather stain remover, such as Punch Salt Stain Remover or Meltonian Stain Remover, which can be effective on water and salt staining.

on washable bedding and fabrics   Rinse in cold water then launder as usual. Dried stains should first be soaked in an enzyme detergent solution (if the fabric is suitable). Marks on white and light fabrics (not nylon) can sometimes be bleached out with a hydrogen peroxide solution (1 part 20 vol peroxide to 6 parts cold water with a few drops of ammonia added). Alternatively, use Stain Devils Coffee & Tea Stain Remover.

Vodka *see* GIN AND OTHER SPIRITS.

Vomit

on carpets With the bowl of a spoon remove the deposit. Flush the area with a squirt from a soda syphon. Blot well. Alternatively sponge the area with a laundry borax solution (15ml borax to 500ml warm water). Rub in the lather from a carpet shampoo solution. Repeat until stain has gone then rinse with warm water with a few drops of antiseptic added. Blot well. Alternatively, after removing the deposit, use the aerosol foam cleaner plus deodoriser, Bissell 'Not on the Carpet' Accident Cleaner. The aerosol cleaner CP-60 is also effective in clearing after-smell.

on mattresses Remove deposit and tip mattress on its side (*see* URINE ON MATTRESSES). Use the Bissell Accident Cleaner as above. Alternatively, holding a pad beneath the area to limit spreading, sponge with a warm solution of washing-up liquid or the lather of an upholstery shampoo such as Bissell Upholstery Cleaner. Wipe over with cold water to which you have added a few drops of antiseptic. Blot well.

on non-washable fabrics Spoon up the deposit. Delicate fabrics or expensive clothes should be dry-cleaned. Sponge the affected area with warm water to which you have added a few drops of ammonia. Blot dry. Alternatively use Bissell Upholstery Cleaner, a deodorising foam suited to leather and colourfast fabrics except velvet, brocatelle and silk.

on washable fabrics and bedding Remove the surface deposit and rinse the area well under a running cold tap. If a suitable fabric, soak and launder in enzyme detergent solution, otherwise wash as usual.

Water marks

on wood *see* PART 3, FURNITURE, REMOVING MARKS.

Whisky *see* GIN AND OTHER SPIRITS.

Wine

on carpets Flush the area with a squirt from a soda syphon or sponge with warm water. Blot well. Rub over area with carpet

I too, had a drink - stain problem, until I discovered mettus!

shampoo solution. Wipe with a cloth wrung out of clear water. Blot well. Repeat until clean. Alternatively use a carpet spotting kit (*see* ADDRESSES). A 50/50 solution of glycerine and water can be left on the stain for up to 1 hour to clear any remaining trace. Rinse off and blot well. Sponging with methylated spirit may reduce old stains.

on non-washable fabrics and upholstery Blot up as much as possible and sponge the area with warm clear water. Blot well. If a mark remains, sprinkle it with French chalk or talcum powder while still damp. Brush off after a few minutes and continue to repeat applications until clear. Dried stains may need lubricating with a glycerine solution (equal parts glycerine and warm water) left for 15 minutes then wiped with a cloth wrung out in warm detergent solution followed by clean water. Alternatively, use an upholstery spotting kit eg Bissell.

on table linen White wine poured over a fresh red wine stain will neutralize it and make it easier to remove. Stretch the fabric over a bowl or basin and pour hot water through it. Otherwise rinse in warm water and soak in a laundry borax solution (15ml borax to 500ml warm water) or heavy duty detergent solution before laundering as usual. Soak dried stains similarly. Dried stains on white fabrics should be stretched over a basin and sprinkled with laundry borax powder before hot water is poured through. Stain Devils Fruit & Wine Stain Remover, or their StainSalts used for the laundering process will take out stubborn stains from white and coloured fabrics. A domestic bleach solution can be used on white cottons and linens without easy care or drip-dry finishes.

on washable fabrics Rinse in warm water and if marks persist, soak or sponge in laundry borax solution (15ml borax to 500ml warm water) or heavy duty detergent solution, where the fabric is suitable, before laundering. For dried marks on white wool or silk (but not nylon) bleach with a hydrogen peroxide solution (1 part 20 vol peroxide to 6 parts cold water). Rinse and launder. On other white fabrics use a domestic bleach solution if the fabric has not a drip-dry or crease-resistant finish. Stain Devils Fruit & Wine Stain Remover, or Stain Devils StainSalts used for the laundering process give good results with wine stains on both white and coloured fabrics.

Xerox ink *see* DUPLICATING INKS.

3

Surfaces – and how to care for them

Regular, correct care of surfaces not only keeps them clean, hygienic and looking good, it also prevents the build-up of many of the stains referred to in PART 2. This section describes the general care needed for cleaning not only various types of surface but also a number of particular items that are likely to be found in many homes.

Acrylic

Baths, basins and shower trays If these are rinsed with warm soapy water and left as dry as possible after use, regular cleaning is made considerably easier. Clean and treat for stains and scratches as described under BATHS.

Furniture Little special care is required for acrylic (rigid plastic) furniture. Regular wiping over with a soft cloth or sponge dampened in a weak detergent solution (use washing-up liquid) followed by rinsing will not only keep it clean but reduce the build-up of static and stop the furniture from attracting dust.

Slight scratching may cause dullness but this can often be removed by rubbing with a soft cloth moistened with a high quality cream metal polish. Stains, too, can often be removed in this way. Wipe off with a moist cloth and buff well. Deeper scratches will need to be rubbed out with fine grade glass paper and finished off with the finest grade wet-and-dry abrasive paper. Afterwards polish with a metal polish.

Utensils Wipe or wash with a soft cloth or sponge dampened in a weak detergent solution as for ACRYLIC FURNITURE above. Clean kitchen utensils quickly as staining can occur easily. Some stains can be removed with a non-abrasive kitchen cleaner or a damp cloth dipped in bicarbonate of soda.

Alabaster

Alabaster is porous and should never be immersed in water but just wiped over with a barely damp chamois leather to remove surface soiling. Discolouration – for example, nicotine stains in an ash-tray – should be wiped with cotton wool moistened very sparingly with white spirit. Never use abrasives or detergents. Buff well with a soft clean cloth or chamois leather. An occasional application of micro-crystalline wax polish eg Renaissance Wax Polish or of Stephensons Olde English Furniture Cream improves the appearance (*see* ADDRESSES). Heavy marking may respond to professional repolishing.

Aluminium

Cooking pans Wash, as soon as possible after use, with hot water and washing-up liquid, using a nylon washing-up brush or scouring pad, such as Scotchbrite, to loosen any food deposit. A steel wool soap pad, such as Brillo, or fine steel wool can be used from time to time to burnish the surface, but rinse thoroughly afterwards as particles of steel wool left in contact with the aluminium can cause surface pitting. Non-stick surfaces or mirror-finished aluminium should never be treated with abrasives. To remove the discolouration that occurs from boiling water, boil up a weak acid solution in the pan (use water plus lemon skin, apple parings or rhubarb), rinse and dry. Never leave food overnight in an aluminium pan as it can cause the surface to pit irrevocably, 15ml of laundry borax in the washing-up water will help to clean aluminium cookware and soaking in a laundry borax solution (15ml borax to 500ml water) will often remove stains.

Teapots The stained interior of an aluminium teapot can be cleaned by filling with hot water, adding 15ml washing powder and leaving for an hour or two. Alternatively use a proprietary stain remover such as Chempro T, avoiding spillage on the outside of the pot. Then brush the inside well with a bottle brush or old (well-cleaned) toothbrush and rinse thoroughly.

ANODIZED ALUMINIUM

Light fittings, trays, trolleys, etc made of anodized aluminium should simply be wiped clean with a damp cloth. A little liquid wax polish on a dry cloth will maintain their gleam. Never use abrasives on them. Anodized saucepan lids can be washed up in the usual way, but they should not be put into a dishwasher. Avoid the use of abrasive cleaners.

Antique furniture

Should you be so lucky as to own some of this, you'll find that its worst enemies are modern developments like central heating. You can mitigate against its effects somewhat by keeping the heating at a constant level of around 18°C (65°F); by avoiding standing valuable pieces near radiators or by keeping them in rooms where the heating isn't on a great deal. The use of a humidifier will also help to prevent the wood drying out too much.

Keeping the finish of antique furniture in good condition doesn't require as much elbow grease as you might imagine. Experts tend to think that it is not a good idea to use modern furniture polishes with added silicones on antique pieces because they tend to give an unnatural finish. Good non-silicone polishes include Antiquax, Kleeneze Antique Furniture Polish, Renaissance Wax Polish, and Stephensons Olde English Furniture Cream (*see* ADDRESSES). You can also make your own from 50g beeswax, shredded into a jam jar, plus 125ml pure turpentine. Stand the jar in hot water until the wax melts to form a buttery paste (do not heat it on the cooker – turpentine is highly flammable). Screw a lid on the jar and use sparingly when required.

Dust antique furniture regularly and remove any greasy marks with a chamois leather which has been well wrung out in a solution of vinegar and water (1 part vinegar to 8 parts water). Buff with a soft cloth until absolutely dry, then polish as usual.

For the removal of more serious marks, eg burns, scratches, watermarks etc, from antique furniture it is best to seek professional advice. However, for a list of such marks, together with instructions on how they may be removed, *see* FURNITURE.

Note For the removal of any marks from French-polished furniture *see* FRENCH-POLISHED SURFACES.

Arborite *see* LAMINATED PLASTIC SURFACES.

Asbestos

Asbestos is a safe material to have in the home provided it is handled correctly. It should never on any account be scraped, cut or sawn as it is the small particles which can cause health hazards. Neither should it be sponged or immersed in water as this softens it and makes the surface break up. At the first sign of damage, discard the article. Seek professional help for removal and disposal in the case of larger items. Work being carried out on existing domestic equipment involving asbestos, eg insulating panels or pipe lagging, should be handled by a professional person.

Baking tins

Badly neglected and greasy tins (except aluminium or non-stick ones) should be boiled up with a strong washing soda solution in a large old pan, then rinsed and dried.

For cleaning advice on aluminium baking tins *see* ALUMINIUM COOKING PANS. Ordinary 'tin' baking tins need washing from time to time though the less often they are washed, the more quickly a non-stick patina is likely to build up. Try just wiping them out with kitchen paper unless you have cooked something like chocolate or treacle cake which tends to stick and needs very thorough greasing of the tins. When they have to be washed, avoid harsh abrasives which damage the coating. After washing, dry them at once or they will rust. A good way to do this is to pop them in the cooling oven.

Non-stick bakeware Should be washed thoroughly taking care not to use a sharp implement or harsh abrasives which might damage the surface. Follow any specific cleaning instructions. Allow it to dry before storing. Some types of bakeware should be washed in clear water; if detergent is used, it becomes necessary to grease the surface. Again, follow the individual manufacturer's advice.

Bamboo

Use a brush or preferably a vacuum cleaner attachment to keep bamboo free of dust. When noticeably dirty, clean it by scrubbing gently with warm soapy water (don't use a synthetic detergent)

with 5ml laundry borax added to each 500ml. Rinse this off with warm salted water (10ml salt to 1 litre water) to help both stiffen it up and bleach it. Wipe with a cloth and allow it to dry naturally, outdoors if at all possible. Polish with furniture cream.

Barbecues

Where possible, follow the manufacturer's care and cleaning instructions. In the absence of specific instructions, clear burnt-on deposits on cold racks by using a stiff wire bristled brush. Betterware Kitchen Carbon Remover, a liquid cleaner, used in conjunction with a wire brush, will remove stubborn or accumulated carbon deposits. Frank Odell Barbecue Cleaner is in aerosol form (*see* ADDRESSES). Cover barbecues stored outside.

Basketware and cane

Try to avoid allowing basketware or cane to become very dirty as it is difficult to get thoroughly clean again. Use a soft brush to remove dust and light soiling. Very dirty sections of unvarnished cane can be rubbed with fine steel wool dipped into a solution of warm water and a little washing soda. Slightly dirty cane should be wiped down with this solution then with cold water to firm it up. Take care not to over-wet the cane. Wipe with a cloth and leave to dry naturally so that it does not warp. Some cane furniture has a clear or coloured varnish finish. This just needs wiping over with a damp cloth from time to time.

Baths

Different types of bath require different care. New baths will normally come with instructions for this which should be followed exactly. All baths will need little special care provided they are rinsed immediately after use with warm soapy water and wiped dry. A daily clean with neat washing-up liquid on a damp cloth or sponge followed by rinsing will do the rest.

Acrylic baths These should not present problems if they are correctly cleaned from the start. Always rinse out well after use, and if necessary wipe the surface with a cloth or bath cleaning sponge, moistened with neat washing-up liquid or rubbed on a cake of soap. Bear in mind when choosing that dark colours are more likely to show up deposits and staining.

Stubborn hard water deposits should respond to the cream cleaning compound Celmac RB90 or Jenolite Bath Stain Remover.

Light scratches can be removed by rubbing gently with a good quality cream metal polish. In the case of deeper scratches or difficult stains, the surface should be lightly rubbed with a very fine grade of wet-and-dry abrasive paper, always using it wet, and working with progressively finer grades of wet-and-dry, or using the same piece which gradually becomes worn away. Finish by rubbing with a cream metal polish.

Bath preparations such as foam baths, bath cubes, etc., are not usually recommended as deposits may remain on the surface after the bath has been emptied, and these soda or acidic deposits can damage the bath.

Glass fibre baths These need special care since the colour is in the form of a surface coating of a 'gel' or resin. If abrasives, even one as fine as silver polish, are constantly used on these they may remove the colour completely, leaving a white patch. In the absence of the manufacturer's recommendations use a washing up liquid eg Fairy Liquid on a sponge and a mild liquid cleaner eg Cleen-o-Pine when necessary.

Vitreous and porcelain enamelled baths Use a proprietary bath cleaner such as Jif, Oz Bath Cleaner, Gumption Cream Cleanser, Cleen-o-Pine liquid, Izal Bath Cleaner or Flash Liquid. Harsh abrasives should be avoided as they will eventually dull the surface of the bath and make it harder to clean. For stains on these surfaces *see* PART 2 BATH STAINS.

Blankets

With correct care, blankets should last for many years. If you can 'rest' them from time to time, stored properly, you will lengthen their useful life. Any blankets not in use should be washed or cleaned then aired and sealed in a polythene bag and placed in a cool cupboard where they won't be crushed. Unless they have been permanently treated against moths, wool and wool mixture blankets should include a moth-repellant sachet in the bag. New blankets will carry a label or swing ticket saying how they should be cleaned.

Many natural and synthetic fibre blankets can be washed, either by hand or in a washing machine. Before embarking on this, it is sensible to check whether the dry blanket will actually fit in your washing machine (and also in the spin dryer in the case of a twin-tub). It may be more sensible to use a local launderette with larger machines since the weight of some blankets could unbalance a smaller domestic model. If you're going to hand wash, using the bath or a large sink, do bear in mind that something like a double blanket becomes an almost unmanageable mass when wet.

Professional cleaning is the alternative and is specially recommended in any case for some blankets. Some laundries and dry-cleaners operate special blanket washing and cleaning services and it's best to use these. Local addresses are available from the Association of British Laundry, Cleaning & Rental Services Ltd., (*see* ADDRESSES). It is not recommended to dry-clean blankets in a coin-op machine, as they must be aired very thoroughly before they are replaced on a bed since any fumes remaining in them are toxic.

Electric Some electric blankets are washable; the manufacturer's instructions for washing should be followed. Never use an electric blanket until it is completely dry. Where an electric blanket has to be dry-cleaned it must usually be returned to the maker who will service it at the same time. This should be done regularly – every three years is the recommended time but check the instructions.

Books

Books need regular dusting to keep them in good condition. When removing one from a bookcase after a period of time, always blow along the top of the closed book or wipe it with a soft cloth to prevent dust falling down between the pages. All books should be either dusted with a feather duster or gone over with a vacuum cleaner attachment once a year whether they've been read or not.

Leather-bound books need special treatment to stop them cracking. Wipe them from time to time with a cloth well wrung out in a warm glycerine-soap solution (whisk soap tablet in warm water to give a lather) then apply hide food, eg Connolly's Cee Bee Hide Food, while still damp, except on dyed leather with no surface protection. Alternatively use Fortificuir (*see* ADDRESSES), a special dressing which both cleans and preserves – follow the maker's instructions. Valuable books may need professional treatment for bookworm, rust or mildew, in which case seek advice from your local specialist bookseller or museum.

Books should be kept out of direct sunlight, in a well ventilated bookcase, in an area experiencing little variation in temperature and humidity.

Bookshelves

Dust regularly and treat according to the material they are made of. Do not allow sticky polish to build up on the shelves and get transferred to the books. Check shelves regularly for signs of woodworm. Where books have got bookworm, treat the shelves too with a good insecticidal spray and polish with an anti-woodworm polish.

Boots *see* LEATHER, SHOES for general care.

Brass

Brass is a copper alloy which tarnishes easily. To clean it use either a metal polish such as Brasso or Duraglit Wadding Metal Polish. Ornamental brass will benefit from the tarnish-reducing film put on it by a long-term polish such as Goddard's Long Term Brass and Copper Polish.

Lacquered brass may become discoloured under the lacquer finish. In this case, remove the finish with either cellulose thinners or nail varnish remover (both highly flammable), or Joy Transparent Paint Remover, then clean. A coat of Rustin's Transparent Lacquer will protect against tarnishing.

Salt and lemon juice mixed to a paste will clean up slightly neglected unlacquered items. To clear dried metal polish deposits from a patterned surface, use a solution of 1tbsp salt and 1tbsp vinegar dissolved in 250ml hot distilled water. Swab over the surface using very fine (0000) steel wool. A soft bristle baby's toothbrush can be used in deep crevices. Work on a small area at a time and rinse and wipe dry before moving on as prolonged contact with the metal can cause pitting. Provided they are small, badly neglected items with the blue/green surface deposit verdigris, can be immersed in a solution of Dax Chemical Brass Tarnish and Verdigris Remover (*see* ADDRESSES). Larger items should be professionally treated.

Brick flooring

To clean brick flooring use a solution of washing-up detergent and scrub with a stiff-bristled brush. Avoid soap, which produces a white crystalline deposit. Mop up the detergent solution, rinse with clear water and wipe as dry as possible. Try to use as little water as possible since an excess brings soluble salts to the surface of the bricks and also lengthens the drying time. Porous brick floors are easier to clean if they are first sealed with a sealer such as Belsealer. For the care of brick fireplaces, *see* FIREPLACES.

Bronze

For regular cleaning, bronze just needs dusting. The occasional application of a very small quantity of oil or brown-coloured shoe polish followed by buffing will improve the sheen and also help prevent the appearance of the characteristic green spots. Badly soiled bronze can be washed in hot soapy water or rubbed over with pure turps or paraffin (both flammable). When dry, brush it with a stiff (not wire) brush that will not scratch the surface.

Brushes

Brooms and cleaning brushes   These pick up a lot of dirt. Remove this regularly – wear household gloves and pick out the larger particles by hand. Wash in a warm mild detergent solution with a final rinse in cold water to stiffen the bristles, then hang up to dry. Do not store brooms and brushes so that they rest on their bristles as this flattens them and destroys their effectiveness. Many come supplied with a hanging hook, if not it is an easy matter to make one by screwing a cup hook into the top of the handle.

Hair brushes   With a comb, remove loose hairs after use. Wash every time you wash your hair by beating up and down gently in warm soapy water. The ventilation hole in a rubber-based brush should be plugged with a small piece of paper or a matchstick before washing. Rinse finally in cold water to stiffen the bristles. Allow the brush to dry naturally away from artificial heat, preferably hanging on a string, otherwise tipped on its side. Do not wet the back of the brush unless plastic – wooden backs tend to swell and ivory and tortoiseshell backs could be damaged irreparably. For special care of ivory and tortoiseshell-backed brushes, *see* IVORY AND TORTOISESHELL.

Paint brushes   Clean according to what paint you have been using – the instructions are usually provided on the tin. Some of the newer oil-based paints can be cleared with water and washing-up liquid or a solution of powder detergent – otherwise white spirit or a proprietary paint brush cleaner will be needed. Use cold water to remove emulsion paint from brushes. If soaking is required, do not stand them directly on their bristles but drill a hole through the handle and suspend them in the liquid from a taut string or nail. There is no need to clean brushes if you are just stopping painting for a short time, for example overnight. Just wrap the bristles tightly in aluminium foil or plastic film until the brush is next required. Exclude as much air as possible from the wrapping.

Cane *see* BASKETWARE AND CANE.

Canvas

Blinds Scrub with washing soap and warm water or a synthetic detergent solution, then rinse thoroughly in cold water. Allow to dry naturally, outdoors if possible, and try to avoid making a crease by hanging the blind over two parallel lines.

Garden furniture see GARDEN FURNITURE.

Handbags Wipe over with a damp cloth and allow to dry naturally. If really soiled, scrub with a nailbrush and soap lather, scrape off any residual foam with the back of a knife, then wipe over with a damp cloth. Do not over-wet. Allow to dry naturally, flexing occasionally to keep it supple. Spray a new or newly cleaned canvas bag with Scotchgard Fabric Protector. This helps to keep it clean and makes future treatment easier.

Tents Only clean if absolutely essential. Tents have a tough, resilient, water-proof coating which will protect against mildew for up to 3 days if you have to fold your tent and steal away without actually having time to dry it thoroughly. When dirty, brush off dirt and any mildew. If washing is essential use a detergent solution and rinse several times to ensure none remains in the fabric, otherwise reproofing won't work. Reproof only if necessary, using the aerosol Dri-Gear for both natural and synthetic fabrics. (*see* ADDRESSES). Most tents will withstand winter storage with just a thorough brushing and airing.

Carpets

GENERAL CARE

Carpets are among the most expensive items when it comes to fitting out a home, so it makes sense to care for them well. Most new carpets come supplied with care instructions. If these are not available ask a reliable retailer or write to the carpet manufacturer to ensure that any treatment you do yourself is of the right kind and will not damage the carpet in any way. RUSH MATTING and SISAL MATTING are dealt with under separate headings in this section of the book.

It is essential to vacuum carpets regularly so as to remove embedded dust and grit (which could otherwise cut the fibres) and to keep the pile in good condition. New carpets may continue to shed fluff over a period. This is to be expected and its removal in no way damages the carpet. Long or shag pile carpets are more difficult to clean and will need regular attention with a carpet rake (available from good carpet retailers). This can be used for lifting the pile to free loose soiling before vacuuming, as well as tidying it after vacuuming. A cylinder cleaner is more effective on 'shag' pile than the upright type. Spots and spills should be removed from carpets as soon as possible after they occur (*see* PART 2 for specific stains).

Cleaning When overall cleaning becomes necessary, there are various methods which can be carried out at home. The carpet can be sent to professional cleaners, or you can call in professional cleaners to deal with a carpet in situ. In situ cleaning is usually preferable for fitted carpets since shrinkage is less likely to occur due to the carpet fixings holding them taut.

Home cleaning can be done either by applying the lather from a solution of dry foam shampoo such as 1001 Foam Carpet Shampoo, Bissell Carpet Shampoo, Sabco Carpet and Upholstery Shampoo, Kleeneze Carpet and Upholstery Shampoo or by the 'steam' method. Dry foam shampoo can be applied using a sponge (which is tiring); by a hand-operated applicator (which is also fairly tiring) or by an electric shampooer which looks rather like a vacuum cleaner and dispenses measured amounts of shampoo at the lift of a lever – these can either be bought or hired by the day. The shampoo dries in powder form, absorbing the dirt, and must be vacuumed clear. Steam cleaners are hired (or you can pay someone to use one in your home). They do not in fact work by steaming but by spraying hot water and a cleansing agent, under pressure, into the carpet pile then extracting it immediately, together with any dirt lodged in the carpet. This is a very effective method of carpet cleaning but more expensive than dry foam shampooing and also more tiring to do if you are operating the machine yourself.

It is important when cleaning a carpet not to over-wet it or colour may come through from the backing and the backing itself may distort. Deep pile carpets may need more than one application. Ideally all furniture should be removed from the room but if it has to be put back before the carpet is completely dry, put small pieces of aluminium foil under any parts that touch the carpet to prevent marks forming.

Cast Iron

Cookware Wash thoroughly and dry immediately to prevent rust forming. Use steel wool or a Brillo Pad. Rinse thoroughly. Any care instructions should be followed.

Decorative ware Decorative ware without a protective coating should first have any rust loosened with a wire brush or steel wool.

Wear goggles to prevent particles flying in your eyes. If necessary brush on a rust remover such as Jenolite Rust Remover & Preventer in the non-drip thixotropic gel form, following the maker's instructions. On embossed and engraved surfaces watch that a heavy brush does not damage the surface. Jenolite Rust Remover & Preventer is also available in liquid form which would allow immersion or brush treatment, so is well suited to these surfaces. To prevent further rusting, apply a thin layer of oil or a film of petroleum jelly. Alternatively use boot polish or a paste wax furniture polish.

Ceilings and walls

Ceilings need attention less frequently than walls although the treatment for both is the same. To clean painted surfaces *see* EGGSHELL, EMULSION AND GLOSS PAINT. To clean vinyl wall coverings *see* VINYL. To clean wallpaper *see* WALLPAPER. To clean or prepare for re-painting first dust the ceiling using a special ceiling brush or the brush attachment of a vacuum cleaner. Wash over any dirty parts with a soft scrubbing brush and warm solution of washing-up liquid, then wipe over the whole ceiling with a cloth wrung out in the solution. Wipe over again with a cloth wrung out in clean water and ensure that all traces of detergent are removed. Use this treatment on tobacco smoke stains, water stains and the heat marks that appear above radiators and chimney breasts prior to painting with emulsion paint. If you are going to put oil-based paint on the ceiling, clean it as described, allow to dry then prime with an aluminium primer or sealer before painting.

Cement and concrete

Wash with a detergent solution or a cupful of washing soda dissolved in a bucket of warm water. Cement and concrete floors are best sealed for easy cleaning and the treatment helps to stop them 'dusting'. After washing thoroughly, remove any ingrained grease marks with Bell 1967 Cleaner, rinse off and let it dry thoroughly. Seal with Belsealer (*see* ADDRESSES).

Ceramic tiles *see* FIREPLACES; FLOORS; TILED SURFACES.

Chandeliers

Turn off the electricity at the mains before any form of cleaning. If possible, chandeliers should be removed from their hanging position for cleaning so that you can handle each piece of glass separately. Use a soft, non-fluffy cloth, preferably fine linen, wrung out in a solution of Handy Andy or washing-up liquid, plus a few drops of ammonia. Rinse, drain and dry each piece with another dry cloth and buff with a soft chamois leather before reassembling. A laborious but effective method of cleaning a chandelier in situ is to rub all over the facets wearing dry chamois leather gloves. The spray cleaner Antiquax Chandelier Cleaner is also used on the hanging fitting. Remember to protect the floor beneath with a polythene sheet to catch the drips.

China, bone

Fine bone china is best washed by hand unless it is specifically marked dishwasher-proof. Use a weak, warm (not hot) solution of washing-up liquid with a soft brush, cloth or mop. Avoid scouring pads, harsh abrasives, bleach or soda which can damage the surface or dull the pattern, especially gold or silver decoration. Use a plastic washing-up bowl in the sink to prevent knocking china on the sink itself. After washing rinse each piece in clear warm water, drain, then dry and polish with a soft tea towel. Do not stack wet pieces on top of each other while draining – a plastic-coated wire rack is a good holder for them. Watch whether any acids such as vinegar or fruit juice seem to affect your china (usually it is the colour that changes) and always wash any pieces so affected immediately. Use a cold water rinse to loosen egg staining and rub over with a damp cloth dipped in salt if it's difficult to get off.

Chromium plate

This is mainly found on taps in the home and on some tubular furniture. Never use steel wool or an abrasive on it as this will damage the thin plating. Wash or wipe with a cloth moistened in mild detergent solution or a multi-purpose liquid cleaner, rinse and buff. Marks should be rubbed with a damp cloth dipped in bicarbonate of soda. Treat corrosion with a metal cleaner such as Silvo, Duraglit Silver Polish impregnated wadding, or 3-in-One Chrome Cleaner (from car accessory shops).

Concrete *see* CEMENT AND CONCRETE.

Continental quilts *see* DUVETS.

Cookers

New cookers come with the manufacturer's recommended instruc tions for cleaning the various parts and it is sensible to hang on to these and follow them as necessary. One good way to keep a cooker clean is to prevent it ever becoming very dirty. Always wipe up spills and splashes on the hob or in the oven as soon as is practicable, preferably while the surface is still warm and the spill has not become hard. For more major cleaning you should first either turn off the electricity at the cooker box or extinguish the pilot light(s).

Electric cookers It is not usually necessary to clean radiant rings or solid plates as these burn themselves clean during use. It is important though, and especially on electric ceramic hobs, to wipe up all spills as they occur to stop them hardening or burning on. With ceramic hobs, use the manufacturer's recommended cleaner. Clean non-ceramic hobs, the back splash and spillage trays with a damp cloth and washing-up liquid solution and wipe dry. Marks should be removed according to the material the surface is made from – *see* ENAMEL and STAINLESS STEEL. The grill should burn off any grease during cooking. Use a soft dry brush on residual soiling and wash a removable grill cover in hot washing-up liquid solution in the sink.

Gas cookers Wash all removable parts in hot washing-up liquid solution in the sink, using a nylon cleaning pad to remove encrusted dirt. Where possible, soak stubborn marks and rub off with a soap-impregnated steel wool pad or a mild abrasive cleaner. Clean the hob itself, back splash, spillage trays and grill as for electric cookers.

Ovens How you clean an oven will depend on its internal finish. Continuous cleaning linings work by vaporizing fat splashes during cooking so that they do not become deposited. The oven needs to be fairly hot to do this effectively so you should try to cook at a high temperature every so often to give the oven a good clean. If necessary the linings can be wiped with a damp cloth. Heavy spillage may fall on to the oven base and needs to be wiped up as soon as cooking is finished. Don't use any form of abrasive cleaner on a non-stick base. High temperature cleaning ovens are found on some electric cookers and the manufacturers' instructions should be followed carefully.

Vitreous enamel oven linings should be cleaned with a liquid or paste cleaner made for use on this surface. For heavy soiling use an impregnated oven-cleaning pad or paste or gel oven cleaner that has been approved by the Vitreous Enamel Development Council (*see* ADDRESSES). Follow the instructions supplied with the cleaner, being careful not to let it touch continuous clean or non-stick surfaces. Work in a well-ventilated atmosphere and wear household gloves.

Oven shelves These are easily cleaned in a dishwasher. (Check that the spray arm can rotate freely once the shelves are loaded in; it may be necessary to remove the top basket.) Take out the shelves after the final rinse but before drying begins, otherwise any stubborn soiling will be baked on. This can be removed with a cloth while the shelves are still warm.

Alternatively, if the oven shelves fit into the sink, soak off the soiling in a warm biological washing powder solution. Otherwise use a mild abrasive cleaner eg Jif on a damp cloth or a worn nylon scouring pad. A soap impregnated pad eg Brillo also gives good results. Burnt-on soiling may require the use of an oven cleaner but check the cooker and cleaner instructions for suitability. The paste/gel types are easier to apply to the bars, and Easy-Off and the SOS Oven Cleaner pad are very effective.

Glass oven doors Check the manufacturer's cleaning instructions; some doors can be removed for easier cleaning at the sink. Soak in hot water and biological detergent. Use a mild abrasive cleaner eg paste or cream Gumption, or Jif on a worn nylon scouring pad for any stubborn marks. Alternatively, clean in situ. Easy-Off or Kleenoff pastes and Mr Muscle Oven Cleaner (spray for a cold oven) are suitable for vertical surfaces. For hinge-down doors, use Sainsbury's Oven Cleaner aerosol. Read the cooker instructions carefully; some advise against spray-type cleaners which could cause warm glass to disintegrate through thermal shock. Clean regularly to avoid a build-up of grime.

Copper

For the general care of copper, *see* BRASS. Copper saucepans should have their exteriors cleaned with vinegar and salt, or a proprietary cleaner such as Duraglit Wadding Metal Polish. They will be lined with either tin or nickel as copper reacts adversely with certain foods and from time to time the lining will need to be renewed.

Corduroy *see* VELVET.

Corian

Corian is a solid, non-porous material with the appearance of marble. It is used for kitchen worktops, sinks, wash basins, bath and shower surrounds. The smooth surface is very durable and needs little maintenance. Wipe with a damp cloth after use, and clean with a washing up detergent solution. Multi-purpose liquid or cream cleaner eg Handy Andy, Jif, or Vim can be used if required. A Scotchbrite pad will clear any light surface scratches and restore its polished appearance. Avoid chopping on this surface, also contact with very hot cookware such as a frying pan or casserole. Most household chemicals, nail varnish and remover will not damage the surface. Clean any spills with detergent and water. Paint removers or drain cleaners may damage the surface and should be rinsed off with plain water immediately.

Cork *see* FLOORS.

Cowhide *see* LEATHER.

Curtain rails, plastic

Remove dust from curtain headings and rails at regular intervals using the suction nozzle of your vacuum cleaner. When curtains are removed for cleaning or washing, wipe down the tracks with a cloth wrung out in a warm solution of washing-up liquid followed by clear warm water. The best results are obtained if the rails can be lifted down and washed or rinsed in a bath since an old toothbrush can then be used to clear the channel of accumulated dust and flies. This is easier if you remove the gliders and soak them separately in a basin of the solution, followed by rinsing. Take care to protect the bottom of the bath with a cloth or an old towel to prevent scratching and try to wet any curtain cords as little as possible or otherwise shrinkage may occur.

If the gliders stick, although apparently free from obstruction, carefully spray the channel with an aerosol lubricant such as WD-40 (don't get it on the curtains). Do not use polish which leaves a sticky surface.

Curtains

Whether curtains should be washed or dry-cleaned depends in theory on the fabric from which they are made. In practice, it is often impracticable to wash even washable curtains at home as their bulk when wet makes them unmanageable and difficult to dry and iron satisfactorily. To keep major cleaning of curtains to a minimum it is important to dust them down regularly using either the brush attachment of a vacuum cleaner or a soft, long-handled brush. Hanging them outside on a fine, breezy day will help to freshen them up from time to time. Lining curtains helps to prevent dirt, condensation and fading from sunlight affecting the main fabric (apart from affording a greater degree of privacy).

As a rough guide, fabrics which can be washed include cottons, linens, man-made fibres and most sheers. Those which should be dry-cleaned include the mixtures of man-made fibres, silks, wool sheers, most pile fabrics and other heavy materials.

When washing curtains at home follow any laundering instructions supplied. Remove all hooks and curtain weights and loosen the curtain heading tapes. Shake them outside to remove dust, or lay them on the floor and run a vacuum cleaner attachment over them. A cold water soak prior to laundering will get rid of a fair amount of soiling. Suit the wash water temperature to the fabric, make sure the detergent is thoroughly dissolved before putting in the curtains, and do not rub or wring. If you are machine washing, follow the wash programme for the most delicate fibre involved. Thorough rinsing is essential for good results. Squeeze out as much water as possible (some fabrics can be spun dry) and hang the curtains over two parallel lines to avoid strain on the fabric. Iron, when necessary, while still slightly damp, working length-

wise on the wrong side. You will need to stretch the curtains gently into shape as you go to avoid puckering along the seams. If a synthetic fabric has become too dry for ironing, it is better to damp it down completely, as sprinkling is likely to leave spot marks. Take the opportunity to clean the windows and sills thoroughly before re-hanging the curtains. When curtains are taken for dry cleaning, tell the cleaner, if possible, the type of fabric concerned.

It is important to wash net curtains before they begin to look grubby, otherwise they become permanently discoloured. Wash separately from other articles and do not exceed the recommended washing and drying temperatures, or permanent creasing will result. The appearance of discoloured net curtains can be improved by the use of the proprietary nylon whitener Dylon Super White, or, in the case of a polyester fibre, Dylon 'Simply White' for Net Curtains.

Decanters and carafes

Decanters and carafes become stained and cloudy either because wine is left in them or because they are put away when damp. If the glass has become etched there is nothing you can do to remove the marks. Otherwise they can be cleaned either by filling with a warm solution of enzyme detergent and leaving to soak, or by pouring in a mixture of vinegar and salt (125ml vinegar to 15ml salt) and shaking from time to time. After both methods, you should rinse the decanter thoroughly in warm (not hot) water and stand it upside down in a wide-necked jug to drain and become thoroughly dry before being stored. Where upside-down draining would be unsafe, eg ship's decanter with wide base, the Manor House Decanter Drier, a gauze tube filled with moisture absorbent crystals, can be hung inside (*see* ADDRESSES). Very bad marks will sometimes respond to soaking in a proprietary stain remover for tableware such as Chempro T.

Diamonds *see* JEWELLERY

Duvets

To keep a duvet clean, always use a coverslip to protect it from the sleeper and also from dirt and spillage. You can buy coverslips or make your own; most people prefer those made from a cotton or a mixture of natural and man-made fibres since completely synthetic ones tend to be very hot and also to slip around. Wash coverslips according to the fabric they are made of – a label should specify this. Deep-dyed coverslips should be washed separately from other laundry until you are sure that no colour runs from them.

Spills on duvets should be mopped immediately to stop them sinking in. If the cover is soiled, push the filling down its channel and tie a piece of white string or cord around the section. Treat according to the type of stain – *see* PART 2. Duvets with synthetic fibre fillings can be washed. This is difficult to do at home as the wet mass is large and unmanageable. It is better to use a launderette which has larger machines or to have it professionally laundered. Washing duvets is not likely to improve the texture of the filling and should be done as infrequently as possible.

Although some duvets with natural fillings can be washed, most require dry-cleaning. This should be done only by specialist duvet cleaners and never in a coin-op machine because of the danger of toxic fumes not being thoroughly aired out of the filling.

For general day to day care, give a duvet a good shake each time you make the bed to keep the filling evenly distributed. Turn it over and from top to bottom from time to time to even out wear.

There must be a better way to clean a duvet than this!

On fine days put it over a washing line or out of a window to allow fresh air to circulate in it.

Earthenware

Earthenware is one of the more common forms of tableware. True earthenware is opaque and, in spite of its sturdier appearance, not as hard nor as resistant to chipping and breaking as bone china. Underneath the glaze it is porous so cracked earthenware will absorb liquids. Some earthenware is ovenproof and usually labelled accordingly, but most tableware should be warmed gently, not placed in a hot oven. Only some types of earthenware can be washed in a dishwasher; they are labelled accordingly. Provided the glaze is not damaged, burnt or stuck-on food will come off after soaking.

Ebony

Never wash ebony as this can damage it. Use a duster to remove surface soiling. Rubbing with a clean cloth regularly and the occasional application of a little furniture cream will keep it in good condition.

Eggshell, emulsion and gloss paint

To clean, first dust the painted area with a soft brush or cloth. Use the brush attachment on your vacuum cleaner or a duster tied over a broom or mop head to reach the higher areas. Using a warm but well diluted solution of washing-up liquid, wash the wall, working from the bottom to the top. This means that any dirty streaks which roll down will reach a clean surface from which they can be wiped easily. Dirt on dirt is much harder to remove. Never use a washing powder as these contain fluorescers which make your washing look brighter but can alter the colour of paint.

Heavily soiled walls should be washed with a weak solution of sugar soap eg Mangers or diluted general purpose household cleaner. Really dirty patches can be removed with neat general purpose household cleaner. After washing, rinse with clear water using an absorbent sponge or cloth. Work in small areas, washing and rinsing each one before you move on to the next. Do not stop until you have completed a whole wall or you will create a line which is difficult to remove.

Note Turn off the electricity at the mains before washing around electrical sockets and light switches.

Electric blankets *see* BLANKETS, ELECTRIC.

Embroidery

If an embroidered article needs cleaning, seek advice from a good dry-cleaner, or the textile department of a museum, depending on its quality. *See* PART 1, EMBROIDERY TRANSFER.

Emulsion paint *see* EGGSHELL, EMULSION AND GLOSS PAINT.

Enamel

Stoved enamel   Usually found on the cabinets (but not always the tops) of appliances such as washing machines, fridges and freezers. These can be kept clean by regular spraying with a cleaner/polish such as Johnson Wax Free Sparkle which you then wipe off. Greasy surfaces can be washed first, using a hot detergent solution. Never polish inside any appliance. Chips and scratches can be touched up with Joy Porcelainit (*see* ADDRESSES).

Vitreous enamel   Found on baths, cooker hobs, oven interiors and the worktops of some appliances. It is glass fused to metal and is more durable than stoved enamel. It can however be scratched with harsh abrasives. To clean vitreous enamel, wash it regularly with a cloth wrung out in detergent solution. Attack marks with a cleaning product such as Flash Liquid, Ajax or Jif. Really stubborn marks may need the use of a special product such as Celmac Liftoff Stain and Scale Remover (*see* ADDRESSES). Chips and scratches can be dealt with as for 'stoved enamel'.

Enamelware

Small items with an enamel coating are called enamelware – things like saucepans, colanders, jugs, mugs and teapots. The enamel may be the vitreous type (*see* above) or simply a sprayed on polyamide finish. Normal washing-up should keep these items clean; in hard water areas it is important to dry them immediately to prevent whitish film forming on the surface. Marks can be removed with Jif, Ajax, Flash or any other cleaner recommended by the Vitreous Enamel Development Council (*see* ADDRESSES). Keep to a cream cleaner such as Jif on a polyamide finish. Stained pan interiors will come clean after soaking in a mild solution of household bleach (5ml to 500ml water). *See also* COOKERS AND PANS.

Fabrics *see* PART 4.

Felt

Felt is very difficult to clean as its dyes are unstable, so water and water-based products like carpet shampoo cannot be used. Felt can be dry-cleaned satisfactorily in a 100% spirit solution but after a couple of times it will begin to look shabby. In any case most dry-cleaners use some water in their solutions. Liquid solvents can be used to remove dirty marks but tend to leave rings or clean patches. The best way to care for felt is to ensure it does not get dirty (line curtains, for example, to reduce soiling). General cleaning can be done with the upholstery tool of a vacuum cleaner and marks are best removed with a soft-bristled or special suede brush.

Fibre glass *see* GLASS FIBRE.

Fire irons *see* BRASS, COPPER or CAST IRON according to the material the fire irons are made of.

Fireplaces

Wherever possible keep to the fireplace manufacturer's cleaning instructions.

Brick With a vacuum cleaner attachment or soft brush remove dust and soot from the brick and then scrub with a hard scrubbing brush and clear warm water. If soiling does not respond, or there are burn marks, try washing down with malt vinegar followed by thorough rinsing.

To remove heavy soot staining *see* PART 2, SMOKE AND SOOT.

Cast iron Remove loose rust scaling with a wire brush or steel wool (wear goggles to protect your eyes), taking care not to brush so hard that embossed or engraved surfaces are damaged. Remove any further rust with a proprietary product such as the brush-on non-drip Jenolite Rust Remover and Preventer following the manufacturer's instructions for applying and neutralizing. To prevent further rusting, it is a good idea to apply a thin layer of oil.

Ceramic tile Wash over the tiles with warm soapy water or a solution of washing-up liquid. If necessary, use a fine paste cleaner, such as Chemico, but not a highly abrasive one nor a harsh brush which could damage the glaze. (Never apply a damp cloth to the tiles while they are still hot as this could cause cracking.) When dry, give a light application of a cleaner/polish such as Mr Sheen, and rub well with a soft duster or clean, dry cloth.

Marble Sponge with clear warm water or a soap solution. Rinse and dry. Polished marble should be cleaned with Bell 1967 Cleaner and polished with Bell Marble Polish or the micro-crystalline wax polish Renaissance Wax Polish. Avoid areas subjected to heat. Worn marble can be improved with Bell Special Marble Cleaner. Chipped or damaged areas can be repaired with Bell Marble 'Touch Up' Pack (*see* ADDRESSES).

Multi-coloured Slate Clean with a cloth wrung out in washing-up liquid. Rinse and buff with a soft cloth. The dry surface can be polished with Bell Marble Polish except for areas subjected to heat.

Riven Slate Scrub with a stiff-bristled brush dipped into washing-up liquid solution. Follow the retailer's advice on stain removal.

Stone Sponge light soiling with clear warm water. Use a scrubbing brush if necessary to remove ingrained particles. For heavier soiling add a little washing-up liquid to the cleaning water then rinse the area thoroughly. Do not use soap or scouring powder which can affect the colour. On badly soiled fireplaces scrub with a strong solution of domestic bleach but take care to protect the surround. In cases of really bad marking it is sensible to consult the fireplace manufacturer about cleaning.

Floors

Different types of flooring need different care. Basic floor care includes having door mats by all exterior doors to prevent dirt being brought into the home, vacuuming or sweeping up loose dirt regularly and always before applying polish, washing regularly where necessary, applying the minimum amount of polish to produce a good shine, removing polish build-up when it starts to get tacky. Where possible, always follow the manufacturer's instructions for maintenance.

Ceramic tiles merely need regular cleaning with a floor mop or cloth wrung out in hot washing-up liquid solution. Rinse with clear water then buff with a soft cloth tied round a mop or broom head. Dirty grouting between tiles should be cleaned with a soft bristled brush. Never apply polish as this makes the tiles slippery.

Cork should have a sealed or waxed finish or vinyl coating to prevent dirt becoming embedded in the otherwise porous surface. Sealed cork just needs damp mopping and the occasional light application of emulsion polish. Waxed cork needs occasional applications of liquid or paste wax polish such as Furmoto Non-Slip Floor Cream or Johnson Wax. If the finish becomes water marked, rub the marks with a cloth dipped in liquid wax polish.

Vinyl-coated cork needs regular damp mopping and very infrequent applications of emulsion polish, eg Johnson Wax Klear.

Linoleum Use a floor mop dampened in a weak solution of general purpose household cleaner and do not over-wet. Once dry, use a liquid or wax paste polish, eg Johnson Traffic Wax Liquid or Mansion Traditional Wax. In kitchens and bathrooms use emulsion polish instead, eg Johnson Wax Klear, as this does not water mark. To remove scuff marks, rub with a cloth moistened in polish.

Quarry tiles Glazed quarry tiles just need mopping with water to which you have added a little liquid general purpose cleaner, such as Ajax. Unglazed tiles will need scrubbing with this solution to remove dirt. Rinse and wipe dry. Unglazed tiles then need to be polished with a liquid or paste wax polish (preferably the non-slip type such as Furmoto Non-Slip Floor Cream).

Where colour has faded, remove the old polish with steel wool and white spirit, wash, rinse and when dry apply pigmented wax polish, such as Cardinal Red Tile Polish, sparingly and buff well to ensure that particles aren't picked up on shoes. White patches on newly laid quarry tiled floors are caused by lime in the concrete sub-floor. In time they will fade and the process can be hastened by washing down with a vinegar and water solution (60ml or 4 tablespoons vinegar to 5 litres water). Do not rinse – leave to dry, and repeat the treatment without polishing until the patches disappear.

Rubber Wash down with a soapflake solution, rinse and allow to dry before applying emulsion polish, such as Furmoto Non-Slip Floor Cream 'Special' or Seel self-shine floor polish. Never use synthetic detergent or solvent-based wax polish as these can soften the surface. To remove scuff marks, follow the floor maker's instructions or use a sparing application of a mild abrasive powder cleaner on a damp cloth. Rinse off quickly with clear water. Damage may occur if done too frequently.

Stone Mop or scrub when necessary with a detergent or washing soda solution (use a handful to a bucket of warm water). Floors in vulnerable areas like kitchens are best sealed with something like Belsealer as this makes cleaning much easier. Before sealing a floor make sure that it is thoroughly cleaned and that any grease marks have been removed – Bell 1966 Cleaner is effective here (*see* ADDRESSES).

Vinyl (sheet and tile) Regular sweeping cuts down on the frequency of thorough cleaning. When this is necessary, damp mop with clear water adding a little general purpose cleaner if soiling is heavy. When dry apply emulsion polish, such as Furmoto Non-Slip Floor Cream 'Special', Johnson Wax Klear or Seel, sparingly. Polish will build up over a period of time and should be removed with the manufacturer's recommended remover or a proprietary floor polish remover, eg Marley Floor Cleaner. Solvent-based wax polish should never be used on vinyl. Scuff marks should be treated with a soft pencil rubber or a cloth dipped in emulsion polish.

Wood (block and strip)   Always keep swept or dry mopped to keep dust and grit from becoming embedded. While a damp cloth can be used to remove sticky marks, never actually wash a wooden floor as over-wetting can seep between boards causing them to warp, or blocks to loosen. If a wax polish has built up on a wooden floor, you can remove it with a cloth and white spirit (turpentine substitute). This is flammable so don't smoke and make sure the room is well ventilated. Alternatively rub along the grain with steel wool dipped in liquid or paste wax, eg Johnson Traffic Wax Liquid or Mansion Traditional Wax. Let the wax harden, then polish thoroughly. Stubborn marks can also be removed by rubbing with fine steel wool. Repolish the floor using a solvent-based polish, such as Mansion Tradiational Wax, Johnson Traffic Wax Liquid or Furmoto Non-Slip Floor Cream. Where a floor has been sealed with varnish or a polyurethane dressing, clean by damp mopping or an occasional application of a wax or self-shining emulsion cleaner, such as Mansion One-Two.

Formica *see* LAMINATED PLASTIC SURFACES.

Freezer

When a freezer has finished defrosting (to do this follow the freezer manufacturers instructions) wash out the interior with warm water and bicarbonate of soda (15ml bicarbonate of soda to each litre water). Do not use a detergent solution which might taint the plastic. On stains use neat bicarbonate of soda on a damp cloth.

If a freezer has defrosted itself while still full of food due to a fault, it may smell very strongly. In this case wash out as suggested above then swab the interior with a solution of Milton 2 Sterilizing Fluid (1 capful to 2.3 litres water) or use Rentokil Fridge Cleaner or Kleeneze Fridge and Freezer Cleaner. Do not use on metal sections. When the inside is dry fill the freezer with screwed-up newspaper and leave it turned off for a couple of days with the door slightly ajar – the newsprint should absorb the smells. Repeat the treatment if necessary.

Clean the outside with a mild detergent solution, rinse and wipe dry. To protect against marks and maintain shine use an aerosol cleaner/polish such as Johnson Wax Free Sparkle or Mr Sheen.

French-polished surfaces

Dust and buff in the direction of the grain regularly. Occasionally apply a very sparing coat of wax polish such as Renaissance Wax Polish or Antiquax paste wax, or a spray furniture polish, and rub in thoroughly. NB If a sweaty hand, placed palm down on the surface for a moment or two, leaves a mark, it is an indication that too much polish has been used. Light marking and a build-up of wax can be removed with a proprietary product, such as Antiquax Furniture Cleaner, or white spirit, applied on a clean soft rag. Moderately serious scratches will need repairing with a home French polish such as Rustin's, following the maker's instructions. Serious damage on valuable pieces should be repaired professionally.

Fur

Natural fur needs care to keep it in condition once it is no longer on an animal's back and able to absorb natural oils. Store fur garments in a loose, closed bag of cotton or silk, hung on a well shaped, long-necked, padded hanger with plenty of space around the garments. If a fur coat is not worn regularly, give it a good shake from time to time and always shake it before you put it on. Put fur into cold storage in summer to revive it and during winter hang it in a cool room where the skin can get plenty of air.

Most coats are moth-proofed and home moth-proofing of any kind should be avoided. If a fur gets wet allow it to dry naturally. Have your fur cleaned professionally, preferably by the furrier who sold it to you. Never attempt any form of stain removal yourself. Obtain professional treatment at once if a tear or split occurs or if you see loose hairs coming out from a fur.

Fur fabric

Most fur fabrics are acrylic, acrylic mixtures or polyester crepe, sometimes knitted and sometimes woven. The vast majority can be washed and garments made from them carry a label giving the appropriate textile wash care information. They should be shaken well while damp and dried naturally. If fur fabric needs dry-cleaning this should be done professionally because cool drying, not obtainable in coin-op machines, will be needed.

Straight pile fur fabric should be brushed while slightly damp but curly pile should never be brushed while damp. In between washing or dry cleaning, keep the pile looking attractive and tangle-free by brushing with a medium-hard brush. Do not allow fur fabric to become too soiled before cleaning.

Furniture

GENERAL CARE

You need to know what your furniture is made of before you can treat it effectively. In general there is less need than most people imagine to polish often – you cannot, after all, feed wood that is only a veneer. Many modern finishes just require wiping over with a damp cloth to keep them clean and no attempt should be made to produce a shine on a piece designed with a matt finish. Many modern pieces of furniture come supplied with a care label. Failing this, it is worth asking the retailer or manufacturer what specific care is recommended for a particular finish.

Specific information on cleaning certain types of furniture is given under the headings ANTIQUE FURNITURE, BAMBOO, FRENCH-

POLISHED SURFACES, GARDEN FURNITURE, GLASS, LAMINATED PLASTIC SURFACES, PAINTED SURFACES, PLASTICS, ROSEWOOD, TEAK and WOOD all in this section.

REMOVING MARKS FROM FURNITURE

Note Where furniture is antique or valuable it is best to seek professional advice for all these marks. For removing any marks from French-polished furniture *see* FRENCH-POLISHED SURFACES.

Alcohol Stains

If alcohol stains do not respond to a good polishing, they can sometimes be removed by rubbing along the grain with a cream metal polish.

Bruise marks

Strip the finish from the whole surface concerned with a paint solvent and varnish stripper eg Strypit. Saturate a piece of blotting paper with water, folding it over several times to make a thick wad and placing over the marks. Leave overnight covered with clingfilm to retain the moisture and swell the wood grain. After removing the blotting paper allow the surface to dry for several hours. Lightly sand the area along the grain of the wood until smooth and refinish according to the surface.

Burns

Where a burn has just caused light discolouration, rub the mark with a traditional cream metal polish, working in the direction of the grain.

On all types of wood (except veneered surfaces), where a burn has roughened the surface, scrape over the rough area with a very sharp knife, taking care not to gouge out unmarked wood (hold the blade as flat as possible). Smooth over with a very fine abrasive paper. Follow with the wet blotting paper treatment as for bruise marks.

With deep burn marks, scrape out the burned wood until you have a clean hole. Fill this with a matching shade of wood filler, eg Brummer Stopping or Rustin's Wood Stopping. Smooth the filler level with the wood surface. The filler will show as it breaks the configuration of the wood grain, but when it has dried its surface can be touched up with a few lines of an appropriate colour of artists' oil or watercolour paint eg umber, ochre, sienna to match the surrounding grain.

For burn marks on a veneered surface, *see* DENTS below.

Dents

in solid wood

Treat as soon as possible while the wood fibres are still loose. Place a little warm water in the hollow to see if the fibres swell sufficiently to raise the dent. If they don't, clean off the wax from the damaged section, lay a piece of damp blotting paper over the dent and apply the tip of a warm dry iron on it. When dry use a similar colour shoe polish to tone in the raised wood. Polish as usual.

in veneered wood

Avoid hard rubbing or wet treatments which could damage the veneer. Dents in veneer usually split the finish so a repair is necessary. Buy a small new piece of similar veneer – an art shop that stocks marquetry sets is a good place to look. Lay the new veneer over the damaged section and with a sharp modelling knife cut an oval shape through both layers, all round the dent or split. Lift off the patch section and remove the damaged oval using a narrow wood chisel; wet it first to soften the glue. NB some modern adhesives may not soften with water; it depends when the piece was veneered. In this case, use the chisel as a scraper to carefully scrape away the adhesive and broken veneer.

Dampen the new piece of veneer to make it pliable, apply wood adhesive to the back and press it into position, wipe off the surplus adhesive before it marks the surrounding wood. After about 10 minutes, smooth the veneer down with a rounded screw-driver handle or other smooth object so that it beds in well. Lay a piece of tissue or brown paper over the repair and weight it down. Leave to dry and harden overnight, then smooth over with fine abrasive paper and colour to match, if necessary, and buff. If the paper sticks to the glue, rub if off lightly with glasspaper or soften the glue with water.

Heat marks

These often look like a white ring. If the surface is not roughened you may be able to burnish out the mark with a cream metal polish rubbed briskly in the direction of the grain. Alternatively, use Topps Ringaway paste.

Ink

Ink is difficult to remove, especially if it's an old stain. Work carefully as the method is fairly drastic and can be quickly overdone. Use a matchstick or cotton wool bud and dab the mark with a household bleach, then blot up with an old cloth or kitchen paper. Several quick dabs are better than rubbing, which will produce light spots. For a large area, or stubborn old marks, try a wood bleach, eg Rustin's, working carefully and following the manufacturer's instructions. This will only work on bare wood so any existing finish should be removed first with a paint solvent and varnish stripper such as Strypit.

Scratches

Light scratches can often be masked using a similar coloured wax crayon or shoe polish. Apply, leave for a while, then buff briskly. Alternatively use a proprietary product such as Joy Scratch Dressing or Liberon Wax Sticks.

Water marks

Try burnishing with a cream metal polish as for heat marks. Where the surface has roughened, use very fine steel wool (000 grade) dipped in liquid wax polish. This method should be used with extreme care on veneered finishes.

COMMON PROBLEMS WITH FURNITURE

As stressed earlier, where furniture is antique or valuable it is best to seek professional help when problems arise. The following advice on care and maintenance refers to 'everyday', humbler furniture of various kinds.

Hinges

Hinges on cabinet furniture often become dry and stiff and if the door is forced open may distort. To cure this, drip a little oil into the top of the hinge so that it runs into the central spindle. Leave it a little time to work and then carefully open and close the door until it swings freely. For hinges that are inaccessible or very stiff use an aerosol lubricant, eg WD-40, but hold a wad of rag around the hinge so that it doesn't get on the surrounding wood.

Sticking drawers

Drawers may stick either because the wood has swollen through damp or because the runners are worn. Where swelling has occurred, remove the drawer and rub soap or candle along the runners or sides. If this doesn't produce any improvement, remove the drawer and carefully smooth the runners or bottom edges with glasspaper wrapped round a wood or cork block. Rub at an angle to

the edge so that you put a slight chamfer on the wood. If the runners are worn they should be replaced with hardwood strips of the correct size.

Garden furniture

Garden furniture, whether it stays out all year or goes into winter storage, needs appropriate care to keep it in condition.

Cane   For the care of cane *see* BASKETWARE AND CANE. Cane garden furniture should always be stored indoors in winter, though not in a heated place as the change of atmosphere can cause it to splinter.

Canvas   Canvas parts on garden furniture are usually rot-proof and should just be wiped over with a damp cloth from time to time. Mend any tears as they occur to prevent complete ripping apart. Canvas parts can be replaced easily as pre-cut seat and back-cover lengths are sold in shops specializing in garden furniture. Fix the canvas with domed tacks on wooden frames; wrap the ends of the canvas around metal frames and sew securely, using a darning needle and heavy twine.

Hardwood   Hardwoods like teak, cedar and iroko will withstand the roughest weather, though prolonged damp may cause discolouration. Marks can be removed with steel wool rubbed along the grain and over-all discolouration may need the application of a wood bleach eg Rustin's – follow the makers instructions. Treat hardwoods with an exterior grade wood preservative, such as Exterior Ronseal Satin Wood Finish or Cuprinol Teak Oil. Hardwood furniture that spends the winter outside should be stood on wooden blocks to prevent the base or feet being permanently damp.

Metal If the tubular type, keep the hinges working well with a drop of household oil. If they have become seized up, use an aerosol lubricant, such as WD-40. Aluminium frame furniture just needs wiping with a damp cloth, wrung out in washing-up liquid solution, to keep it clean. Grease marks can be removed by adding a tablespoonful of laundry borax to this solution. Corroded parts should be scrubbed with the solution, then rinsed and dried. To restore the shine rub with dry steel wool, always working in one direction to avoid scratching. When dry, dust it down and apply two coats of Joy Transparent Paint.

Tubular steel furniture usually has a rust-resistant finish but the risk of rust can be kept at bay by rubbing down with a smear of oil or grease, particularly during winter. Cast-iron and steel furniture usually has an enamel-painted finish and just needs wiping over with a damp cloth or a hose-down. Hinges will need occasional oiling and any chipped areas should be treated with a proprietary rust remover, such as Kurust or Jenolite Jelly Rust Remover & Preventer, before repainting with exterior grade enamel.

Plastic Wipe over with a damp cloth and use a mild detergent solution on dirty spots.

Softwood When new, seal wooden framed furniture by treating with a polyurethane lacquer, such as Translac Polyurethane Clear Varnish or Rustin's Yacht Varnish, to protect it. Rustin's Danish Oil can be used for a natural, low lustre finish, or their Teak Oil for a slight sheen. For maximum protection, treat the undersides as well. Dirty furniture should be scrubbed down with detergent solution, rinsed and dried before applying the seal. Marks can be removed from the bare wood by rubbing along the grain with fine steel wool. With the exception of the Yacht Varnish, you will need to reapply the seal each year to keep the furniture in good condition.

Gilding

Cleaning is only necessary when discolouration occurs, otherwise just dust. To clean, treat with a cloth dipped in warm turpentine or turpentine substitute. Do not heat the turpentine in a pan directly over heat but place it in a bowl of hot water as it is highly flammable.

Glass

Glass surfaces, items like glass topped tables and glass-fronted bookcases should have the glass cleaned with window cleaner, eg Windolene, SOS Glass Works or an aerosol furniture polish; apply it sparingly then buff free of smears.

Glasses Wash in warm water, using your usual washing-up liquid. Rinse in the same temperature water, drain and dry with a soft linen cloth or chamois leather. Cotton cloths tend to leave fluff. Always wash glasses separately, using a plastic bowl or rubber mat in the sink. Do not store glasses stacked one inside the other as they may stick. They are best stored the right way up as the top rim is the most delicate part and prone to chipping. Take particular care when drying stemmed glasses as the stems are easily twisted off. Everyday tumblers can be washed in a dishwasher, but fine crystal and cut glass should always be washed by hand to avoid the 'etching' (cloudy marking) that can result from continual cleaning in a dishwasher.

Mirrors see MIRRORS.

Oven-to-table ware Wash-up in the usual way. Stuck-on food will usually come off after soaking. Some can be put in a dish-washer.

Windows see WINDOWS.

Glass fibre baths and sinks *see* BATHS, GLASS FIBRE.

Gloss paint *see* EGGSHELL, EMULSION AND GLOSS PAINT.

Goatskin

Rugs Should be cleaned professionally as goat's hair is very brittle and can break away at the base if washed at home. Coats are specially treated to avoid this. Follow the care label's advice.

Gold

Gold articles should be cleaned with a special impregnated polishing cloth, eg Goddard's Long Term Silver Cloth, kept for this purpose; then buff with a soft dry chamois leather. Gold chains should be washed in a bowl of warm soapy water using a soft-bristled brush if necessary to get into the links. Rinse and allow to drip dry before rubbing over with a chamois leather. Try not to put any strain on the chain as a link could break. Heavily tarnished gold requires professional cleaning.

Gold leaf

No other treatment than careful dusting is required unless the gold leaf becomes discoloured. In this case dab gently with a solution of 10ml ammonia to a cup of warm water. Rinse with clear water and dry carefully with a soft cloth. Touching up with a 'gold leaf' paint will always be noticeable.

Grasscloth

Wallcoverings made from grasscloth are difficult to clean without damaging the grasses. Use a vacuum cleaner tool to remove surface dust and do not stand furniture against them which could rub and mark them. Grease marks may never come off but it's worth doing a test with an aerosol grease solvent, eg Goddard's Dry Clean, to see if it will damage the grasscloth – if not, have a go but take care.

Hessian-covered walls

The dyes used in hessian wallcoverings are usually weak and not stable so the best method of cleaning is to remove embedded dust with a vacuum cleaner tool. Hessians should never be hung in a kitchen or bathroom because of the cleaning difficulties. For marks never use water or stain removers but try rubbing over them with a piece of slightly stale bread.

Horn

Care involves dusting with a soft cloth and occasional washing. Use only warm water as horn can soften in high temperature water. Wash carefully in clear distilled or softened water. Don't use detergent: it destroys the surface polish which makes horn impermeable. Dry with a soft cloth. Polish with a metal polish – the best for this purpose is Solvol Autosol paste polish (from car accessory shops). Do not polish drinking vessels without washing them thoroughly afterwards.

House plants

Plants that live indoors tend to be the type that started life in the tropics. Basically their needs consist of warmth, light, air and food. Some people think they also need company and conversation but these will depend on the temperament of the owner rather than the type of plant. Plants do not need excessive heat and most will die in temperatures over 24°C (75°F). A cool spot is fine for most, but what should be avoided is constant change of temperature – for example in rooms where there is no heat by day and a coal fire at night.

Plants are more likely to thrive if they get plenty of natural daylight and will be happier in rooms where white walls and ceiling can help to reflect it. Artificial light, provided it is fluorescent, will also help plant growth. Some fresh air is necessary for an indoor plant to flourish and in good weather it is a good idea to stand them by an open window or door or even give them a short spell completely outside. Guard against draughts though and never give them doses of really cold air. Note that fumes from gas, solid fuel appliances and dirty oil heaters can damage house plants, as can fumes from freshly applied paint.

Food must be supplied by fertilizers once the plant has used up the supply of plant food present in the potting medium. Plants need only be fed during the growing season and should be left to rest when dormant. Many house plants from shops and nurseries come with a care-label attached and you can ask a knowledgeable seller to give you additional tips. If you want to grow a house plant successfully, it would be sensible to invest in a book giving information on what different varieties require.

Like other household items, plants will get dusty; the dust will form a film over the plant and prevent it from breathing as well as eventually spoiling its appearance. Dust can be removed by syringing or sponging the leaves with clear water. Very dirty leaves, for example on a rubber plant, should first be dusted with a soft cloth. You can buy proprietary leaf shiners which give glossy leaves back their sheen but these should only be used sparingly and occasionally. Pruning, training and repotting should be done when necessary.

Indoor plants *see* HOUSE PLANTS.

Iron, pressing

The sole plate of an iron may become marked by starch or scorching. To remove these marks, rub the iron over a damp piece of loosely woven cloth held taut on the corner of a table or ironing-board. Alternatively, use the proprietary product Vilene

Iron Cleaner. Very fine steel wool will remove bad marking but avoid scratching the soleplate and never use on a non-stick surface. When removing these marks from a steam iron, hold it in the ironing position so that the dislodged particles do not fall into the steam vents and clog them up.

Steam irons will eventually become furred-up in hard water areas though this can be considerably reduced by using de-mineralized or distilled water, preferably purchased from a chemist (do not use the water collected when defrosting the fridge which, although de-mineralized, could be contaminated). Although some models of iron require professional defurring, on others you can do the job yourself, using a proprietary scale remover such as Scale Away, Descalite or Oz Iron Cleaner and following the manufacturer's instructions.

Iron, wrought

If new and without a painted finish, give decorative wrought iron used indoors a protective treatment by applying a lacquer, eg Rustin's Transparent Lacquer. If this produces an unpleasantly shiny result, tone it down with a light coat of wax polish. As an alternative to lacquer, an application of Rustin's Satin or Matt Black Finishing Paint would protect the surface. Where rust has got a hold, use a proprietary rust remover, eg Jenolite Rust Remover & Preventer, following the maker's instructions.

Hinges which are corroded should be treated with penetrating oil, eg 3-in-One Penetrating and Easing Oil, to make them work efficiently again. Once it has penetrated, wipe the oil off, clean the area with turpentine substitute and apply a lubricant such as WD-40.

Ivory

Ivory may be any colour from white to yellow. Daylight will help to maintain a good creamy colour and sunlight has a bleaching effect, but avoid strong sunlight through glass on ivory as the heat produced can cause drying out and cracking. Extreme cold is dangerous too, particularly for ivory-backed hand mirrors, as the ivory can contract and crack the glass or the ivory itself.

To maintain a high polish on ivory, dust it regularly with a soft cloth, using a soft brush to get into the crannies on carved and intricate pieces. Ivory should never be put in water as after a period it will develop hairline cracks even though no initial damage seems to have been done. To keep them in good condition, give mirrors, brushes and other pieces an occasional light application of almond oil using a soft cloth. Clean them from time to time with a cotton-wool swab dampened in white spirit. This also maintains the polish and helps keep the surface free of the acids which cause discolouration. Valuable antique ivory should not be treated with white spirit.

Ivory is semi-porous and will absorb spots of toilet preparations, scent or hair spray. These should be wiped off immediately or the resultant stains may require professional attention. To wash an ivory-backed hairbrush use a warm soapflake solution on the bristles (never detergent or ammonia). Beat the bristles up and down in this but do not immerse the ivory back. Rinse the bristles in clear warm then cold water, wipe the back and tap the bristles on a towel to remove as much water as possible, then gently dry them, facing downwards, so no damp gets into the ivory. Avoid drying them by artificial heat, such as in an airing cupboard or on a radiator, which could cause the ivory to crack.

Never wet ivory knife handles: soak the blades in a jug of hot washing up water and dry individually. Store in acid-free colourless tissue (*see* ADDRESSES).

Jade

Jade should be handled with care and any non-jewellery items dusted carefully. Fingermarks and surface soiling can be removed with a soft-bristled brush dipped in warm soapy water (don't use synthetic detergent). Rinse the item quickly in clear warm water then dry it with a soft cloth and buff with chamois leather.

Jet

Shiny jet should be buffed occasionally with a soft dry cloth or chamois leather. Dull jet should just be dusted as necessary. Never use water, polish or abrasive on either shiny or dull jet.

Jewellery

Jewellery needs care if it is to remain in perfect condition and, if real, keep its value. All good jewellery should be cleaned professionally once a year by a reputable jeweller who, to protect his reputation, cannot afford to do a bad job. This will not only clean the jewellery but ensure that it is checked for worn links, loose stones, damaged claws, etc. It is sensible for insurance purposes to have good jewellery revalued once a year while it is being cleaned; the value of jewellery continues to increase and inadequate insurance might mean you would be unable to replace a treasured piece.

Regular home care for jewellery is necessary to maintain sparkle. Porous stones such as turquoise and opal should never be immersed in water but just polished with a soft dry chamois leather, using a dry, soft, bristle brush to clean claw settings. Pearls, too, should never be washed. The oils from your skin will help to maintain their gleam, so wear them as much as possible (but not while applying make-up, scent or hair lacquer), and rub them gently with a chamois leather from time to time. Marcasite jewellery should also be polished with a soft brush, then rubbed gently with chamois leather and should never be washed.

Hard stones, which includes amethysts, diamonds, rubies and sapphires, can be cleaned in a warm solution of Fairy Liquid and scrubbed gently with a soft toothbrush or eyebrow brush. Rinse in lukewarm water, then dip quickly into surgical spirit to remove any remaining detergent film before draining on absorbent paper and buffing with a chamois leather. These stones can also be cleaned by immersion in a jewellery care kit, eg Goddard's. Gin, despite popular myth, is not a satisfactory substance for cleaning precious stones.

Certain stones require extra special care. Emeralds, for instance, are softer than the other precious stones and can chip easily. They can be cleaned in a warm solution of Fairy Liquid, as above, but care should be taken. Although diamonds are very hard, they have a grain similar to wood and a hard knock could split them. Diamonds may also scratch other diamonds if stored close together.

Always wash jewellery in a plastic bowl with an old towel or piece of absorbent cloth placed in the base. This will prevent pieces getting damaged, or disappearing down the plughole. But put the plug in – just in case.

Kettles

How you clean the exterior of your kettle, be it electric or the hob type, will depend on what material it is made of – *see* ALUMINIUM, COPPER, ENAMELWARE, STAINLESS STEEL, etc. Cleaning the interior is more of a problem, as fur builds up and makes the kettle less efficient. Ideally you should deal with fur as soon as it starts to form rather than wait until there is a thick layer. There is a choice of descaling agents on the market, but it is important to check the kettle manufacturer's instructions to see if a particular type or brand is recommended. Descalers come in both powder and liquid form and are easy and not messy to use. Most are suitable for aluminium, brass, copper or iron, but not recommended for zinc, galvanized or enamelled metal. The proprietary product Scale Away can be used for kettles in most materials including those in plastic such as Kemetal. Basically, you just add the descaling agent to warm water in the kettle and leave it to fizz until the scale dissolves, neutralize, then rinse out several times. Follow the maker's instructions and wear household gloves.

Knives, kitchen

Kitchen knives have either stainless steel or carbon steel blades. For care of stainless steel blades *see* STAINLESS STEEL. Carbon steel blades should be washed and dried immediately after use to prevent food acid stains or rust building up. Where staining has already occurred, rub the blades with a nylon scouring pad and, if this does not remove the marks, rub them with the flat end of a wet cork dipped into an abrasive cleaning powder, eg Vim, or use wet-and-dry abrasive paper. Rub vegetable oil over blades to protect them while stored. Handles tend not to be dishwasher-proof, particularly if made of wood which is likely to split. Plastic handles can usually be put in a dishwasher safely.

Lace, discoloured or yellowed

Antique lace For cotton lace that is heavily discoloured or yellowed, professional treatment should be sought since the method of bleaching required is a highly professional one. For badly discoloured silk lace, unfortunately little can be done in the way of professional treatment. Never use any home bleaching method for either.

Some improvement can, however, be effected by soaking antique cotton or silk lace in clear cold distilled or softened water over a period of several hours. The lace should be laid as flat as possible on a piece of white nylon net so that it can be lifted out of the water without strain being imposed on it. Change the water several times as the discolouration starts to lift from the lace. Finally raise the lace on the net and slide it, wet, on to a smooth surface – a sheet of polythene is ideal. Make sure there is plenty of water still in it and pull it carefully to shape, then blot it well with a towel. The lace can be pinned out using rustless pins. Allow it to dry naturally in an airy place, away from direct sunlight. On no account should the lace be pressed or ironed.

Machine-made lace Today's machine-made laces are mainly man-made fibres. Discoloured nylon lace which does not respond to normal laundering with a mild detergent in warm water, may be improved by the careful use of a proprietary nylon whitener, eg Dylon Super White. In the case of a polyester fibre, eg Terylene, use Dylon 'Simply White' for Net Curtains. Most modern curtain nets are made in a polyester fibre.

Lacquer

The term lacquer is used to describe the transparent sealing coat applied to metals such as brass or copper. It is also used for objects lacquered under the old Chinese system which should be cleaned simply by dusting.

Metal sealing lacquer also needs no care apart from routine dusting. If areas of lacquer get rubbed off or chipped, the metal will eventually start to discolour. The only remedy for this is to remove all the lacquer with a proprietary lacquer remover, eg Joy Transparent Paint Remover or nail polish remover (both flammable), clean the metal according to type, then re-apply a layer of lacquer.

Laminated plastic surfaces

Laminated plastic surfaces are now found all over the home, in kitchen, bathroom, bedroom and living room.

Formica and Perstorp Warerite are the tough laminates, used in areas of heavy wear. These will stand up to kitchen worktop use though you should not chop directly on them nor put anything on to them straight from the cooker.

Wiping with a damp cloth will keep the surface clean and washing with water and mild detergent should remove most marks. For obstinate food and drink stains, apply neat washing-up liquid, or a non-abrasive liquid surface cleaner such as Cleen-o-Pine or Ajax, and rub gently with a damp cloth. Persistent stains may need careful rubbing with a slightly abrasive cream cleanser eg Chemico or Gumption, which should also clear pencil, ball point and felt-tip marks. Always rinse with clear water and polish with a soft cloth. A few drops of vinegar on a wash leather, or a proprietary window cleaner eg Windolene will remove and avoid smears on the surface.

Melamine-faced chipboard is another plasticized surface usually used in doors, vertical surfaces and shelves. It's not as strong or durable as the laminates and is more easily stained. Clean as above.

PVC (polyvinyl chloride) surfaces are often found on self-assembly bedroom furniture. They are tough and scratch resistant but their construction – a sheet of pvc foil stuck to the solid panel with adhesive – means that if the corners become unstuck you can peel the whole sheet off. Clean with a damp, soapy cloth, but do not over-wet.

Lampshades

Lampshades are meant to cast light in an attractive manner and they will not do this if they are allowed to collect dust and dirt. Dust lampshades regularly as part of your routine cleaning. From time to time before they begin to look soiled, clean them according to what they are made of.

Buckram   A stiff brush will be needed to remove dust. Marks can be removed by rubbing the shade with a cloth dipped in turpentine. Go over the whole shade to avoid a patchy effect.

Plastics   Sponge with a cloth wrung out in warm, soapy water, then in clear water. If the whole lampshade is washable, immerse it and swish round in soapy water, then in clear water; pat dry with a soft cloth.

Vegetable (imitation) parchment   This should never be wetted or it may disintegrate. Dust with a soft cloth or brush and rub gently at any marks with a soft, clean india rubber.

Vellum (parchment)   Wipe over with a solution of 1 spoonful of soapflakes in an equal amount of water plus 2 spoonfuls of methylated spirit, shaken together. Rinse with a cloth moistened in methylated spirit. Polish with Renaissance Wax Polish (*see* ADDRESSES). *See also* VELLUM.

Lavatory

Lavatory pan   Scrupulous and regular cleaning is essential to keep germs at bay. A lavatory pan should be cleaned every day by brushing around the pan with a lavatory brush followed by flushing. Keep the brush clean by regular washing in hot soapy water, followed by rinsing in cold water to which you have added a few drops of disinfectant. At least once a week clean the pan with one of the powder or liquid products sold for this purpose. Do not leave either type in contact with the surface longer than recommended otherwise penetration may occur through worn areas or cracks in the glaze, resulting in discolouration.

Never use a powder lavatory cleaner with another cleaner as toxic gases could be released. If a cleaner is left in the lavatory overnight be sure to flush it in the morning before the lavatory is used. Consider using in addition to an ordinary cleaner a flush block, which is sited in the cistern and contains detergent which is flushed around the lavatory after each use.

The removal of hard water staining may require a stain and scale remover such as Celmac RB90 or, for particularly stubborn marks, the chemical treatment Celmac Liftoff. Follow the manufacturer's instructions.

Lavatory seat Keep a special cloth for cleaning purposes and use it, dampened in a warm water and disinfectant solution, to wipe the lavatory seat on top and underneath every day. At least once a week give the same treatment to the outside of the pedestal.

Lead

Garden ornaments Some people like the natural weathered appearance of lead and prefer to leave it without attention. It can be cleaned by scrubbing with turpentine until the desired colour is reached, then hosing down. Heavily soiled pieces may need treatment with a household scouring powder, eg Vim.

Leather

Leather keeps the animals whose skin it is protected from the elements. If looked after correctly, it can do the same for you and should give years of wear.

Bookbinding see BOOKS.

Chamois Wash by hand following the manufacturer's instructions. Where none exist, prepare a warm soapflake solution and squeeze the chamois leather in it to release the dirt. Rinse once, in warm water with 5ml of olive oil added and swished around to disperse it. This helps to retain its soft texture. Squeeze out as much moisture as possible. Pull into shape and hang in an airy place away from artificial heat. Hand flex the leather during drying to maintain its suppleness.

Clothing Leather clothing is often described as 'washable', which in fact means 'spongeable' as it should not be immersed in water. Most clothing comes with care instructions from the manufacturer and these should be followed. All leather clothing will need professional cleaning every 3–4 years, including re-tinting and re-oiling. If it gets wet during wear, wipe with a clean cloth and allow to dry naturally. Store in a cotton cover or unsealed plastic bag in a cupboard, using a well-padded hanger.

When a leather garment is new or newly cleaned, it is sensible to apply a coating of Scotchgard Suede and Leather Protector, to protect it against weather and spills. Test first. Surface soiling can be removed from washable leathers with a soapy swab (use glycerine toilet soap or a soapflake solution, not a synthetic detergent), then wipe with a clean damp cloth before hanging to dry. As the garment gets older, an occasional application of hide food eg Connolly's Cee Bee or Hidelife will keep it looking good.

Desk tops   Providing the leather is of the washable type it can be wiped over from time to time with a damp cloth which has been rubbed across a tablet of glycerine toilet soap or wrung out in a warm soapflake solution. While damp, apply a hide food, eg Connolly's Cee Bee or Hidelife, sparingly. Ink marks can usually be removed if sponged immediately with water; ballpoint ink is more likely to respond to milk. Antique-finish leather desk tops should just have an occasional application of hide food to clean, preserve and protect the surface against staining.

Fake   Clean with a soft cloth moistened in warm soapy water – not synthetic detergent which could damage it. Rinse with clear water and buff with a soft cloth. Scotchgard Suede and Leather Protector can be used to protect new or newly cleaned simulated suede finishes.

Gloves   Most leather gloves are washable and special glove shampoos are available. Otherwise, use a warm soapflake solution. Wash gloves on your hands rubbing gently to remove dirt. Take them off and allow to dry naturally. When almost dry pull them back on to your hands to restore the shape. Doeskin gloves should not be rinsed as the residual soap helps keep them supple. After washing, press them between two towels to remove excess wetness, then dry naturally.

Furniture   Dust leather furniture regularly and give it an occasional application of hide food eg Connolly's Cee Bee or Hidelife to prevent cracking and help protect against stains. To freshen up the surface, remove dirt with a soft damp cloth, which has been rubbed across a tablet of glycerine toilet soap or wrung out in a soapflake solution; never use synthetic detergent which may damage the surface. Do not rinse as the residual soap will help the leather to stay supple. Finish off by wiping over with a soft damp cloth. Where leathers are specifically not 'washable' take professional advice on their care.

Luggage   The natural oils will keep leather luggage in good condition at first but you will then need to apply hide food occasionally. After use, loose dirt should be brushed off the luggage and the leather wiped over with a damp cloth, which has been rubbed across a tablet of glycerine soap or wrung out in a warm soapflake solution. Finish with a cloth wrung out in clear water and pat dry. Odd marks may respond to rubbing with eucalyptus oil. Bashed and worn suitcases can have their appearance improved by rubbing over with a solution of 10ml vinegar, 2.5ml ammonia and 500ml water. When dry, rub the leather over sparingly with castor oil, then polish with a good quality furniture cream such as Mansion Traditional Furniture Cream.

Reptile skin   This, used for shoes and handbags in general, just needs dusting. An occasional application of special reptile skin dressing, eg Meltonian Neutral Shoe Cream – sold in a jar – or Connolly's Cee Bee Hide Food will keep it gleaming – always rub it in gently, in the direction in which the scales lie.

Shoes and handbags   Ask about care when you buy a new pair of shoes and, if a special product is required, buy it there and then. An initial application before you wear the shoes will help provide a protective surface against dirt, wet and stains. Many recommended shoe polishes not only clean, but also contain soluble dye stuffs to restore faded colour and cover up scuff marks eg Punch Shoe Cream with Scotchgard. Regular applications will keep shoes looking good and restore the natural oils that get lost during wear. Handbags don't take such a drubbing as shoes but need similar care. Take care that all polish is well rubbed into a handbag or it may come off on your clothes. For this reason, don't choose the pigmented polishes.

Patent   Do not allow patent leather to become excessively cold or it may crack. Dust it with a soft cloth and apply patent leather dressing from time to time eg Punch Patent Glow aerosol. If used only infrequently, apply a thin layer of petroleum jelly all over and wipe this off before each use.

Suede clothes   It is possible to buy washable suede and it is worth paying extra for this since actual laundering is possible. With new or newly cleaned suede an initial application of Scotchgard Suede and Leather Protector or Swade Guard prevents colour rubbing off and also provides a protective surface that can be wiped lightly with a damp cloth to remove surface soiling. Test first.

When suede does become dirty, or if rain spots don't disappear despite brushing, wipe the entire section over with a cloth well wrung out in clear cold water and allow to dry naturally. Then brush up with a wire brush and it is likely that all marks will disappear. Alternatively, there are suede cleaning cloths or blocks for this purpose, eg Swade Groom or Swade Aid; these are particularly useful for removing soiling along wear creases. Where this home treatment fails (and before the garment is heavily soiled), take the garment to a specialist suede cleaner who will not only clean it but restore any lost colour and oil.

Suede shoes When necessary, clean with a nailbrush dipped in warm soapy water. Don't use detergent which can damage the finish. Finish with the nailbrush dipped in cold water, but do not over-wet. Blot with a dry cloth and allow to dry naturally. Alternatively, use a proprietary product such as Punch Suede & Fabric Shampoo following the maker's instructions. When suede shoes get wet allow them to dry naturally, then use a rubber or nylon suede brush to remove dust and raise the nap. Fresh mud should be scraped off while still wet and soiling blotted with a damp cloth.

Once cleaned, or better still when new, protect suede shoes with a protective dressing such as Swade Guard or Scotchgard Suede and Leather Protector. Fading can be improved with an over-all application of appropriately coloured suede dressing such as Meltonian Suede Spray or Punch Suede Renovator, both of which contain the waterproofing agent Scotchgard.

Light bulbs

Always switch off electricity before removing a light bulb and, if the light has been on, wait for the bulb to cool down. Hold it by the cap and carefully wipe over with a well wrung out damp cloth. Dry thoroughly with a soft cloth or duster before replacing. Never attempt to clean a bulb which is still in its socket. Fluorescent light tubes should be removed and cleaned in the same way.

Linoleum *see* FLOORS.

Lloyd Loom Furniture

Clean dust from the weave using a hair dryer or the blower attachment of the vacuum cleaner. (The hair dryer should be used at the lowest possible heat setting; ideally, use a dryer with a 'no-heat' setting.) Wipe lightly across the weave using a brush dipped in a warm washing-up detergent solution. Avoid over-wetting. Finish with a cloth rinsed and well wrung out in clear warm water and allow the furniture to dry naturally.

Marble

For the care of marble fireplaces *see* FIREPLACES. For general care of table tops and mantlepieces marble just needs to be dusted with a soft brush and washed over when necessary with warm soapy water (not detergent), rinsed and buffed with a soft cloth. Colourless wax polish can be applied sparingly to coloured marble to give it sheen, but never to white marble as it can cause yellowing. Surfaces used for food preparation should never be waxed. Dirty marble can be cleaned with Bell 1967 Cleaner and polished with Bell Marble Polish. Bell also make a special cleaner (*see* ADDRESSES) for badly marked old marble, but where damage or staining is extensive, professional cleaning is a better bet.

Mattresses

Spring interior   Turn over or swing round to reverse head and foot once a week when new, then quarterly after a month or so. This helps the filling to settle. Use the handles and if possible get someone to help you. Every so often, brush the mattress and the base below it to remove dust and fluff. Do not use a vacuum tool for this as it may dislodge the filling. Take care not to pull out tufts or buttons. It is possible to purchase white cotton covers for protecting the mattress. These are removable for laundering.

Foam   Foam mattresses with a layered construction should never be turned. Single density foam mattresses should be turned once a month. Cleaning of dust and fluff can be done with the crevice tool on a vacuum cleaner.

Melamine

Tableware can be cleaned by normal washing-up. Although the manufacturers do not recommend putting melamine tableware in a dishwasher, it is usually perfectly safe to do so. Avoid abrasive cleaners; stained cup interiors can be cleaned by using the special Uniglan cleaner (*see* ADDRESSES) or a mild solution of baby's bottle sterilizer, eg Milton 2. Staining will be greatly reduced if cups and beakers are washed as soon as possible after use. *See also* LAMINATED PLASTIC SURFACES.

Metals

Metals should be cleaned carefully to avoid abrading their surface. It is important to use the correct polish for a particular metal as metals fall into two categories – hard and soft – and polish for a hard metal such as brass will damage a soft one such as silver. If you are uncertain which metal it is, in the case of a long-neglected object, play safe and use Duraglit Wadding Silver Polish. For how to clean particular metals *see* ALUMINIUM; BRASS; BRONZE; COPPER; GOLD; PEWTER; SILVER; STAINLESS STEEL.

Microwave Ovens

Where possible, follow the manufacturer's cleaning and care instructions. Wipe the interior surfaces after each use to clear excess condensation or general food spillages. Fat splashes or stubborn food deposits can be removed with a specialist cleaner such as Microwave Clean, Mr Muscle or Oz Microwave Oven Cleaner. To remove a build up of odours, heat an uncovered bowl of water to which some lemon peel has been added on a high power setting for 3 to 4 minutes. Wipe away any resulting condensation. Clean the outside with a multi-surface liquid cleaner and wipe dry.

Mirrors

Glass Glass mirrors can be cleaned in the same way as windows (*see* GLASS), using a proprietary window cleaner according to the directions and buffing up with a soft cloth. For bathroom and kitchen mirrors it is possible to cut misting by wiping the mirror with an anti-mist product, eg Holts Anti Mist, obtainable at cycle and garage accessory shops. Hair spray marks can be removed with a cloth moistened in methylated spirit, followed by an application of window cleaner.

Melinex (mainly used commercially) scratches easily so should be cleaned with a very soft cloth or feather duster.

Mother-of-pearl

Cutlery handles Because mother-of-pearl is slightly porous, cutlery handles are vulnerable to acid and vinegar staining and, during washing up, grease in the water may be absorbed and produce dark stains which cannot be removed. This cutlery should be washed in warm soapy water, separately from other items. Try not to immerse the handles.

Ornaments Clean with a paste of powdered whiting (obtainable from art shops) and water. Rub it on gently then wash off with warm soapy water. Alternatively, use a white cream furniture polish.

Tables and work-boxes When cleaning items with inlaid mother-of-pearl sections avoid the sections which should be cleaned separately with a non-abrasive polish such as a white furniture cream, eg Stephensons Olde English Furniture Cream. Where the mother-of-pearl is inlaid or superimposed on papier-mâché (which may well look like wood), take professional advice on cleaning. Professional attention is also essential for restoring articles that are stained or have lost their natural lustre.

Nickel

This metal tends not to be widely available today, having been replaced mainly by stainless steel and chromium plate. No special polish is available, so clean it with a proprietary silver polish, eg Silvo.

Non-stick surface cooking pans

Keep the manufacturer's care instructions when you buy a non-stick lined cooking pan and follow them. Some non-stick pans can be washed in a dishwasher and the instructions will give guidance on this. In general, hand washing-up in hot water and washing-up liquid will clean most of them although some require clear water only. Do not use steel wool, scourers or abrasive powders on a non-stick surface. Usually, wooden or plastic spoons etc., rather than metal, should be used with non-stick pans.

From time to time rub a non-stick surface over with a wet nylon or plastic cleaning pad or stiff sponge. This will remove the build-up of grease. Heavy food stains can be removed by boiling up a solution of 1 cup water, ½ cup liquid bleach and 30ml bicarbonate of soda for 5 minutes, then wash the pan as usual and grease the surface lightly to recondition it. *See also* PANS, and, for non-stick bakeware, BAKING TINS.

Nylon

Fur see FUR FABRIC.

Fabric see PART 4.

Utensils see PLASTICS.

Oil paintings

Because oil paintings are not covered by glass, when you dust them you will be dusting the painted surface itself. When dirt builds up to a degree that needs cleaning you should seek professional treatment if the picture is in any way valuable. For less valuable works you can buy a special picture cleaner – Winsor & Newton's Artists' Picture Cleaner – from art shops and follow the maker's instructions exactly. It can be used on varnished and unvarnished pictures but will remove varnish so you will need to re-apply aerosol Artists' Picture Varnish – again obtainable from art shops – when cleaning is completed. It is important to use the picture cleaner carefully and stop when colour starts to come off the picture on to the cotton-wool pad used.

Onyx

Onyx is porous and will absorb even perspiration from the hands, so it should be handled as little as possible. Dust it regularly and use a damp cloth, well wrung-out in water to remove any surface soiling. Light marks can be removed by rubbing with a cloth moistened in methylated spirit. Drinks spilled on to an onyx surface will be absorbed unless wiped up immediately and the onyx will subsequently require professional regrinding and re-polishing.

Ormolu

Ormolu is bronze overlaid with gold leaf and is used as decoration on furniture. If the surface becomes dulled, clean with a swab of cotton-wool well wrung out in a solution of 10ml cloudy ammonia in a cup of warm water. Don't let it touch any wood sections; it may be necessary to mask these with cardboard cut-outs. Rinse well with a cloth wrung out in clear water, then dry with a soft cloth. Never use metal polish or lacquer.

Oven *see* COOKERS.

Painted surfaces, washable

Walls Dust and wash using a diluted solution of washing-up liquid. Work from the bottom upwards to avoid streaks. *See also* CEILINGS AND WALLS; EGGSHELL, EMULSION AND GLOSS PAINT.

Woodwork Light soiling can be removed with an aerosol all-purpose cleaner/polish such as Mr Sheen or Johnson Wax Free Sparkle. Really grubby patches should be wiped with a cloth wrung out in a solution of washing-up liquid, then wiped over with clear water. On stubborn, greasy marks, use Flash, in solution, Handy Andy or Ajax Liquid. Never use an abrasive as this will dull the finish and remove some of the paint film. Lustre-finished painted wood, particularly if gilded, needs special care and gentle wiping with a weak solution of washing-up liquid.

Pans

Burnt The safest way to remove burnt food from a pan is by soaking. Fill with a solution of enzyme detergent powder in hand-hot water. Leave this to soak for a few hours then bring it to the boil. Remove the softened deposit and clean the pan according to what it is made of. Only if repeated applications of this method fail will it be necessary to use an abrasive. *See also* ALUMINIUM, COPPER, ENAMELWARE, NON-STICK SURFACED COOKING PANS and STAINLESS STEEL.

Papier-mâché

Dust papier-mâché items regularly. Wipe over occasionally with a cloth wrung out in soapy water, wipe with clear water and dry. Protect ornamental articles with a light application of furniture cream, eg Stephensons Olde English Furniture Cream.

Patent leather *see* LEATHER.

Perspex

For general care, use washing-up liquid solution, rinse and dry thoroughly. A light application of a cleaner/polish eg Mr Sheen will maintain shine and help repel dust. Light scratching can be removed by buffing with a soft cloth moistened with a little cream metal polish. Wipe off and buff well.

Pewter

Pewter must be cleaned regularly, otherwise oxide scale develops which tarnishes the surface and has to be removed professionally. For a soft glow on your pewter just wash it in soapy water and dry it well with a soft cloth. Any grease marks can be removed with a little methylated spirit on a cotton-wool swab before washing. For a real shine use a polish suited to pewter, eg Duraglit Wadding Metal Polish, always rubbing round not across the article.

Piano keys

Ivory This can discolour with age and use. Bad discolouration will require professional scraping. On pianos which are not very valuable, however, you could try a solution of equal parts of methylated spirit and warm water applied on a well squeezed-out pad of cotton-wool, followed by buffing with a soft non-fluffy cloth. Mild discolouration will often bleach out if the piano lid is left open for the sun to shine on the keys and plenty of air to circulate. For general care, wipe the keys over with a chamois leather well wrung-out in warm water to which you have added a few drops of vinegar. Don't let water trickle between the keys; wipe dry immediately.

Plastic These will not discolour in the same way as ivory. Dust them frequently and clean with a chamois leather well wrung out in warm water to which you have added a few drops of vinegar. Wipe dry.

Picture frames

Gilt or gilded Dust regularly. If discolouration appears, rub over the frame with a cloth dipped in turpentine or turpentine substitute. Branded wax gilt, Treasure Gold, can be bought from art shops and used to touch up any damaged spots. *See also* GILDING and GOLD LEAF.

Wooden Use a little furniture cream to polish regularly and buff well.

Pillows

Foam Foam pillows have a fabric cover over them. Where a spill has stained the cover but not penetrated into the foam, the cover can be unpicked and removed for washing. The foam interior is very soft and can tear easily if handled roughly. Don't leave it exposed to light or use it until it is sewn back into its own cover. Minor marking on a foam pillow can sometimes be removed by sponging with warm soapsuds followed by sponging with clear water and mopping with a towel. Do not over-wet and dry the pillow in its cover or a pillowslip near the top of a warm airing cupboard away from direct heat. If the foam is saturated by spillage, complete immersion may be necessary. Leave the cover on and using warm, soapy water, squeeze the pillow gently, taking care not to twist or wring it. Rinse until the water is completely clear and gently squeeze out as much water as possible. Wrap the pillow in a large towel and press out further moisture. Dry the pillow very thoroughly as described above. This may take some time but persevere until drying is complete.

Natural fibre Pillows filled with down or feathers should be aired regularly, out-of-doors in summer. They can be washed by hand but, unless you own a large spin drier, this is not recommended, as drying otherwise takes an incredibly long time. Some laundries will wash pillows for you. Do not wash pillows with worn covers or damaged seams. Pillows filled with natural fibres should not be dry cleaned as it is difficult to remove all the toxic fumes from them.

To wash a pillow by hand use either the bath or the wash tub of a top loading washing machine. Use a soapflake or mild detergent solution. Squeeze the pillow well in the suds so that the filling is thoroughly penetrated. Rinse two or three times in warm, clear water. Squeeze out the excess water then wrap round in a spin dryer, to balance the weight, and spin for not more than 30 seconds. Do not use a tumble dryer as you could damage both the dryer and the pillow.

Finally, peg the pillow lengthwise on a line out-of-doors. Take it down and shake it occasionally, then re-peg on the opposite side. It may take several days before it is completely dry, in which case bring it in at night and rehang in the morning. Air it thoroughly in a warm place before putting it on a bed.

Synthetic fibre Pillows filled with Dacron or polyester can be washed either by hand or in a front-loading machine – a launderette machine which is larger than a domestic model is better able to cope with the size. Follow the pillow maker's instructions for drying. Synthetic-filled pillows should not be dry-cleaned.

Plants, house *see* HOUSE PLANTS.

Plastics

Plastics are among the easiest surfaces to keep clean and in general a wipe over with a mild detergent solution followed by rinsing will do the trick. Cleaner/polish sprays like Mr Sheen and Johnson Wax Free Sparkle are good for maintaining a shine on surfaces which are not used for food preparation. For more specific information on the care of different plastics, *see* ACRYLIC; LAMINATED PLASTIC SURFACES; MELAMINE; POLYSTYRENE; FLOORS, VINYL.

Polystyrene, expanded

This is usually found in the form of ceiling tiles. Dust them carefully with a duster tied over a broom head, or use the brush attachment on a vacuum cleaner. Take care not to depress the surface. In a kitchen they may be greasy, in which case sponge as necessary with a warm, mild detergent solution, avoiding pressure. Rinse with clear water and allow to dry thoroughly.

PVC (polyvinyl chloride) *see* LAMINATED PLASTIC SURFACES.

Porcelain

Real, hard-fired porcelain is not porous so can be washed in a detergent solution. Do not immerse any pieces that have cracks or chips. Rinse in clear water and dry thoroughly. Do not wash porcelain items in a dishwasher.

Pottery *see* EARTHENWARE.

Quarry tiles *see* FLOORS.

Radiators

Most radiators have a painted finish – *see also* PAINTED SURFACES. Dust, or especially in the column type, use a vacuum cleaner tool. When necessary, wipe over with a cloth wrung out in mild detergent solution. For bad soiling use a heavy duty household cleaner such as Flash in solution. Cover the floor below a radiator while cleaning. Rinse thoroughly and wipe dry.

Refrigerators

Inside Most new refrigerators have an automatic defrosting facility and just need occasional cleaning. Older models have to be defrosted either by pushing a button or by switching off at the electrical socket, and this should be carried out as soon as ice begins to build up round the frozen food compartment. Follow the maker's instructions. Once all the frost has melted, empty the drip tray and wipe the frozen food compartment dry.

Non-automatic models require more frequent cleaning, ideally every 2–3 weeks, following defrosting. Automatic models still need regular cleaning to maintain their hygienic condition, but at less frequent intervals. Disconnect the electricity supply. Remove all the shelves and fitments. With a solution of 15ml bicarbonate of soda to 1 litre warm water, wipe over all the inside surfaces, except for the metal sections. Dry well with a soft cloth. Alternatively use Rentokil Fridge Cleaner, a sanitizing fluid which clears grease and inhibits growth of mould and algae. Wash the fitments at the sink, using a washing-up liquid solution and rinsing well before drying and replacing.

Metal sections   Wipe with a cloth wrung out in clear water.

Outside   Wipe over the outside with a warm detergent solution and rub dry. Occasionally apply some aerosol cleaner/polish such as Mr Sheen or Johnson Wax Free Sparkle.

Rosewood

For basic care of wood *see* WOOD. Use occasional sparing applications of good quality wax furniture polish, eg Renaissance, Mansion Traditional Wax, Antiquax. Do not use silicone polishes or sprays which tend to produce a sticky surface. Remove surface soiling and fingermarks by wiping over with an absorbent cloth wrung out in a warm solution of 1 part vinegar to 8 parts water, but do not over-wet. Wipe dry and repolish when the surface is completely dry so that there is no danger of sealing in moisture and creating a white bloom.

Rubber flooring *see* FLOORS.

Rush matting

Vacuum rush matting as if it were ordinary pile or cord carpet. Treat stains with a solution of warm water and washing soda; occasionally sponge or scrub over the matting with soap and warm water. Lift occasionally and vacuum up the dirt which will have fallen through any holes. Otherwise it can turn to mud when the matting is wetted.

Sheepskin

Coats   Do not allow a sheepskin coat to become very soiled before sending it for professional cleaning. When new or newly cleaned, spraying with a protective solution such as Swade Guard, or Scotchgard Suede and Leather Protector, will help prevent it marking. It is best to wear a scarf to guard against soiling during wear. If the collar does become soiled, however, the wool side can be freshened up with a dry shampoo for hair. Home cleaning of the skin side can be done with Swade Groom or other proprietary suede cleaners. Test first.

Rugs Provided the wool is not very long, the best treatment for a sheepskin rug is to wash it yourself at home. For an average size rug you will need 175g soapflakes, 50ml olive oil, 50ml glycerine, 125g fine oatmeal and 125g flour – the last four ingredients are for feeding and softening the skin. Boil the soapflakes and olive oil in a pan with 1 litre water, stirring well to emulsify the oil.

Add this emulsion and the glycerine to enough water to wash the skin. The wash water temperature should be warm (about 40°C). Wash the skin well, then drain off the wash water. Do one deep rinse but do not rinse out all the soap which helps to keep the skin supple.

To dry the skin, squeeze out surplus water with your hands, then rub both sides with dry towels. Hang up to dry, bearing in mind that it will be more likely to come up in good condition if not wringing wet when hung. The best place is an outdoor clothes line on a sunny, windy day. Failing this; put it on a rack over the bath. When the skin is almost dry, rub equal quantities of flour and oatmeal into the back to make good the loss of tanning materials. When the rug is completely dry, comb or brush the wool.

Shoes

Leather and Suede see LEATHER, SHOES.

Plastic see LEATHER, FAKE.

Showers

Shower head Limescale deposit blocking the holes can be cleared by soaking in a descaling preparation such as Descalite Kettle Scale Remover or Scale Away.

Shower tray see BATHS

Silk wall hangings

These should always be cleaned professionally in situ. Do not allow them to become too dirty before having them cleaned. To keep them in good condition avoid hanging them in direct sunlight or in any room that is damp. If they have to be stored do not fold or crease them or they will crack.

Silver and silverplate

Silver and silverplate tarnish easily through exposure to certain gases in the atmosphere. Utensils for food also tarnish through contact with the sulphur in things like egg yolk, fish, green vegetables and salt. Silver and silverplate used for eating can be washed-up in the usual way, either by hand or in a dishwasher. From time to time it will need polishing to restore the shine as will other silverware around the house.

Silver polishes come in paste, liquid, impregnated wadding and impregnated cloth forms. Some polishes are described as long-term and contain tarnish inhibitors which extend the time before repolishing is needed. Long-term polishes aren't as good at cleaning heavily tarnished silver as the non-long-term types and are best used after one of the latter has been used for the actual cleaning. There are also liquids in which articles are cleaned by immersion. They should not be used on plated pieces which have any damaged plate. Never use dip type liquids near stainless steel sinks and surfaces, which can be stained indelibly by them.

A home-made silver polish can be produced by placing a 10cm wide strip of alumimium foil across the base of a plastic washing-up bowl, and laying the silver on top of it. Put a handful of washing soda in the bowl and cover the silver with hot water. When the bubbling stops, rinse the silver and buff it with a soft cloth. It may be necessary to repeat the treatment when there is heavy tarnishing. Stored silver should be put in acid-free tissue paper (*see* ADDRESSES) or tarnish-proof bags (available from jewellers) and kept in an air-tight box in a dry place.

Sinks

Sinks need general care to keep their outlets working properly and specific care according to what material they are made of.

GENERAL CARE

To clear any solidified grease dissolve a handful of washing soda in 500ml boiling water and pour it down the outlet. Never put solid matter which could block the waste pipe or drain down the sink outlet. To clear a blocked drain that does not respond to the washing soda treatment, use either a proprietary drain cleaner such as Kleenoff Drain Cleaner, following the maker's instructions, or a sink cup plunger, remembering to block off the overflow. Serious blockages may need treating from the U bend.

SPECIFIC CARE

Acrylic-type   Use a cream cleaner such as Jif to avoid a build-up of stains. Do not use harsh abrasives or scouring pads. Lemon juice or vinegar should remove limescale deposits. Stubborn marks respond to the cream cleaner Celmac RB90.

Fireclay   Use a cleaner recommended by the Vitreous Enamel Development Council (*see* ADDRESSES) as being suitable for general or bath cleaning. Where discolouration has occurred through the glaze wearing down, use a mild solution of household bleach.

Stainless steel   Rinse regularly after each use and dry with a cloth to prevent water spots forming, especially in hard water areas. Surface soiling can be removed by rubbing with neat washing-up liquid on a damp cloth. Never use harsh abrasives or scouring pads on stainless steel. From time to time polish with a proprietary product such as Prestige Copper & Stainless Steel Cleaner, Jonelle Stainless Steel & Hob Cleaner or Wenol Metal Polish (*see* ADDRESSES) following the manufacturer's instructions.

Vitreous enamel   Clean with a product recommended by the Vitreous Enamel Development Council (*see* ADDRESSES) for general or bath cleaning. Use a plastic washing-up bowl to prevent chipping, but always make sure that no gritty particles collect underneath or they may scratch the enamel.

Sisal matting

Vacuum regularly (but not when wet or muddy) and lift occasionally so that you can sweep up the particles of dirt that have fallen through any holes. Most types of sisal matting can be cleaned (but preferably as infrequently as possible) with a dry foam carpet shampoo such as 1001 Foam Carpet Shampoo, but it is sensible to check with the maker of the matting before attempting this. Apply the lather gently with a soft-bristled brush or sponge. Take care never to over-wet the matting; securing it round the edges before shampooing helps to prevent shrinkage. Always allow to dry naturally. Stains should be removed immediately; dried marks often won't come out. Sparing applications of carpet shampoo or aerosol stain removers as applicable are most efficient in this respect.

Slate

Dust or sweep regularly and scrub when necessary with a detergent solution followed by rinsing. Heavily soiled surfaces can be cleaned with Bell 1967 Cleaner. Grease marks can be removed with a wet poultice of Bell Special Marble Cleaner (*see* ADDRESSES). You can polish with a light application of wax polish, eg Ronuk Wax Polish, and buff with a soft cloth. Never polish floors which could become slippery, fireplace surrounds where heat would make the wax deposit sticky, or areas such as larder shelves where food is around. *See also* FIREPLACES, RIVEN SLATE.

Spectacles

Spectacles that aren't cleaned regularly hinder rather than help vision. Wash them frequently in warm, soapy water and dry carefully with a soft cloth. Polish the lenses daily with a soft cloth, holding the frame at the top and bottom of each lens to avoid any strain. If they become misted from cooking or spotted from rain, wipe them dry and clean by breathing on both sides of the lens and polishing with a soft cloth. Proprietary lens cleaners are available from opticians.

Stainless steel

Although tough and relatively stain free, stainless steel still needs a certain amount of care. Permanent staining is caused by contact with a dip type silver cleaner; hot grease or fat splashes may produce permanent rainbow coloured marks. Mineral salts in tap water can cause a white film if stainless steel is not dried thoroughly, and prolonged contact with vinegar and other culinary acids also causes staining. A proprietary cleaner, such as Prestige Copper & Stainless Steel Cleaner or Jonelle Stainless Steel & Hob Cleaner, will remove most marks with the possible exception of dip type silver cleaner and heat marks.

Pitting may occur as a result of prolonged contact with water, so never leave stainless steel saucepans or cutlery soaking overnight, or undried longer than necessary. Common salt, neat bleaches, and undissolved detergent can also cause permanent pitting. Stainless steel can be kept clean by washing, either by hand in a solution of washing-up liquid or, in the case of items like cutlery – providing they are 'dishwasher-proof' – in a dishwasher. Take care to avoid spoons nesting one inside another – spread them around the cutlery basket. Occasional polishing with Prestige Copper & Stainless Steel Cleaner, Jonelle Stainless Steel & Hob Cleaner or Wenol Metal Polish maintains mirror finish stainless steel. For care of stainless steel sinks *see* SINKS.

Steel

Ordinary steel requires regular cleaning and occasional burnishing with fine steel wool or a medium emery cloth, though the latter can be difficult to obtain. On ornamental articles, rub over a little furniture cream such as Mansion Traditional Furniture Cream to protect them from rust. Neglected items and light rust marks can be cleaned with a wire brush or steel wool. Wear goggles to prevent particles flying in your eyes. Heavier rusting will probably need treatment with a proprietary rust remover such as Jenolite Rust Remover & Preventer which is available in liquid form for immersion/brush on, thixotropic gel for brush application, or as a jelly for use on small areas (*see* ADDRESSES).

Stone

Fireplaces see FIREPLACES, STONE.

Floors see FLOORS, STONE.

Table linen

Table linen should be laundered according to the type of fabric from which it is made.

Teak

For basic care *see* WOOD. Teak is a hard wood that on factory-finished furniture needs very little special care, apart from regular dusting. Teak products such as Johnson Wax Living Wood Teak Wood Care, Topps Teak Cream, Rustin's Teak Oil and Cuprinol Teak Oil are available, but only sparing and occasional use (about 2–3 times a year) is needed to clean the surface and maintain the teak's matt gleam.

Teapots

Teapots should be washed up by hand or machine according to the material from which they are made. A small teapot spout brush can be bought to clean down the spout. When stains build up to an unacceptable level, rub pottery and china with a damp cloth dipped in salt or bicarbonate of soda then rinse thoroughly. Alternatively treat stains with a proprietary cleaner such as Chempro T, Kleeneze Tea and Coffee Stain Remover or Uniglan (*see* ADDRESSES) (but not in the case of aluminium teapots with the exception of Chempro T) following the manufacturer's instructions. Silver teapots should have their interiors rinsed out with either clear water or a mild washing-up solution followed by rinsing. For cleaning the outside *see* SILVER. For stains on aluminium *see* ALUMINIUM.

Terrazzo flooring *see* FLOORS, CERAMIC TILES.

Thermoplastic flooring *see* FLOORS, VINYL.

Ties

Most men's ties are in a man-made fibre from the polyester, acrylic or acetate groups, or one of the natural fibres such as silk, wool or cotton. Since it is not easy to remove isolated stains without leaving a ring mark on most of these fabrics, it is a good idea to spray new, or newly cleaned, ties with a fabric protector such as the aerosol Scotchgard Fabric Protector. (Try a test area on the back of the tie and allow it to dry first.) This will prevent spills and splashes penetrating the fibres for long enough to allow them to be easily removed.

If stain removal becomes necessary, an impregnated stain removal pad, eg Spotkleen, can be very effective on grease and wine marks and is not as likely to leave a ring mark as the liquids. When full cleaning becomes necessary, follow any guidance given on the tie label. Unless labelled 'washable', professional cleaning is advised for silk and other expensive ties since pressing can be very tricky and the dyes used may not be fast to laundering. If you have difficulty in finding a dry-cleaner who will accept ties, consult the Association of British Laundry, Cleaning & Rental Services (*see* ADDRESSES).

Hand washing is preferable for most types of washable ties. Use a warm mild detergent solution, eg Dreft or Stergene, and squeeze the tie to remove soiling. Avoid rubbing since it frays and distorts the interlining. Rinse well and use a final cold rinse for all but wool. Roll in a towel to remove excess moisture then dry naturally.

Pressing a tie Polyester and other man-made fibres may not require pressing. For other fabrics, position the tie, wrong side up, on the ironing board. Make sure that the bias cut interlining is crease free, then slip a cardboard shape or 'former' up inside the wide end of the tie so you can press without transferring the shiny seam lines to the face of the tie. Silk, with the exception of tussore (wild) silk, needs a warm iron and is best pressed while still slightly and evenly damp. Wild silk should be completely dry. Most tie fabrics scorch easily so press over a clean dry tea towel.

Tiled surfaces

Aluminium wall tiles Wipe over with a hot solution of washing-up liquid, rinse and dry with a chamois leather. Buff up with a soft cloth.

Ceramic wall tiles Clean as aluminium wall tiles. In a shower area where lime deposits may build up, clean with white vinegar wiped on neat, left on for 10 minutes to dissolve the lime then washed off. Stubborn deposits may need a cleaner made for this purpose and obtainable from tile merchants. Check its suitability for the finish involved eg glazed or matt. Grouting between tiles can be cleaned with a soft brush dipped into a solution of domestic bleach, but take care not to loosen it. Protect the floor and surrounds to prevent spotting. Badly marked and damaged grout is best scraped out and the gaps re-grouted.

Floor tiles see FLOORS, CERAMIC, QUARRY OT VINYL TILES.
Mirror wall tiles Wipe down with a chamois leather or soft absorbent cloth wrung out of a solution of 15ml white vinegar in 500ml warm water. For further care see MIRRORS.

Tin

Kitchen tinware such as roasting tins, pastry cutters, graters, etc. should be washed immediately after use in a hot solution of washing-up liquid. Rinse, then dry (a cooling oven is a good place). Discard tin items once they become rusty. *See also* BAKING TINS.

Toilet see LAVATORY.

Tortoiseshell

Keep items out of direct sunlight as this tends to dry them out. Preserve the lustre by buffing with a soft clean duster, and the occasional use of a little jeweller's rouge applied on a soft cloth and buffed well. Clean by wiping with a cloth dampened in soap solution. Do not use any oily or wax preparations as these will attract dust; avoid allowing perfume or hair spray to fall on to tortoiseshell. White marks sometimes appear on neglected tortoiseshell which has been left in the sun, exposed to heat or over-wetted. These need expert attention.

When washing a tortoiseshell-backed hair brush, smear the back with a sparing application of non-abrasive polish, such as Mansion Traditional Furniture Cream, to protect it. Avoid immersing it in water as this could cause it to distort. Wash the bristles gently by beating into a warm soapflake solution; rinse them in warm water and then in cold to stiffen. Tap on a towel to remove excess moisture and leave to dry, bristles down, on a dry towel. When dry buff the back with a soft cloth or chamois leather.

Imitation tortoiseshell is usually made from celluloid or opaque horn. It needs only dusting and an occasional wipe with a damp cloth.

Upholstery

Upholstered items rarely receive the same care as clothes although they get similar, and sometimes heavier, wear. All upholstered items should be thoroughly dusted once a week, preferably using the soft brush attachment of a vacuum cleaner: if possible use the crevice tool for around the seat edges and other hard-to-reach sections. Once or twice a year, it is a good idea to precede this treatment by beating the furniture all over with a short smooth cane, taking care that every area is dealt with. This loosens dust that has become embedded.

Keep items out of direct sunlight as far as possible and ensure that reversible cushions are turned over once a week to give even wear. Clean upholstery before it becomes heavily soiled, following manufacturer's care instructions wherever these are available. Loose covers should be removed and either dry-cleaned or washed carefully according to type. If washed, put them back on the piece of furniture before they are completely dry to ensure a good fit and prevent shrinkage. Complete the ironing with the covers in position; be sure to use a cool iron on foam upholstery.

Where covers cannot be removed you can either call in specialist cleaners to attend to them in your home (which is expensive) or, if suitable, clean them yourself with an upholstery shampoo such as Bissell, 1001 Foam Carpet Shampoo or Sabco Carpet and Upholstery Shampoo, following the maker's instructions. On Dralon (acrylic) velvets use only the lather from the shampoo to prevent over-wetting, which will cause the cotton in the backing to shrink. Always work in the direction of the pile, never against it. Always test home treatments on an unseen area, allowing the section to dry completely for inspection before deciding to proceed.

Unless labelled 'washable', chenilles, tapestries, velours, velvets and fabrics containing silk, wool or viscose should be dry-cleaned.

Leather upholstery see LEATHER. FURNITURE.

Vinyl and plastic upholstery just need dusting with a soft-bristled brush and wiping with a damp cloth. More thorough cleaning can be done with a cloth wrung out in a warm solution of soapflakes followed by clean water. Alternatively use a vinyl upholstery cleaner designed for car seats, such as Turtle Wax Upholstery Cleaner. Don't over-wet the surface.

Vellum

Remove loose dust with a feather duster or soft cloth. Wash carefully with swabs of cotton-wool wrung out in warm water, taking care not to over-wet. Wipe over with cotton-wool wrung out in milk and leave this to dry on the surface or polish with Renaissance Wax Polish. Never use a leather preservative.

Velour

Velour is expensive and difficult to produce. It should be dusted from time to time with the soft brush attachment of a vacuum cleaner and any cleaning should be carried out professionally. Home cleaning is not advisable unless it is one of the new spongeable varieties, when it could be treated with a product such as Turtle Wax Velour Cleaner.

Velvet

Velvet may be made of silk, cotton or man-made fibres. All should be dry-cleaned unless their instructions specifically state that they can be washed. Washable velvets can usually be washed in a machine and in some cases tumble-dried. Non-washable velvets should be dry-cleaned professionally. Acrylic velvet, such as Dralon, should be cleaned using only the lather of an upholstery shampoo to avoid overwetting the backing which might shrink due to the cotton content. Alternatively it can be dry-cleaned, but tell the cleaner it is acrylic and therefore a process involving strong heat should be avoided.

Vinyl

Miscellaneous   Raincoats, bags, shower curtains and roller blinds should be cleaned by wiping over with a mild detergent solution and avoiding the use of abrasives.

Sheet and tile flooring see FLOORS, VINYL.

Upholstery see UPHOLSTERY, VINYL AND PLASTIC.

Wallcovering   Wash with a mild detergent solution, working in an upward direction. Rinse with clear water. Do not over-wet. Work from the bottom upwards, as trickles of dirty water are easier to remove from a clean surface.

Vitreous enamel   Sometimes referred to as Vitramel; *see* ENAMEL, ENAMELWARE.

Warerite   (Perstorp Warerite) *see* LAMINATED PLASTIC SURFACES.

Wallpaper

Ordinary wallpaper   needs careful cleaning or you may damage the surface. Dust it with a soft brush or vacuum cleaner attachment, but take care not to press hard on embossed papers or you may spoil the pattern. Rubbing with a soft india rubber or slightly stale bread may prove effective on small soiled areas, such as around light switches. Never wash paper or the colours may run and the paper become loosened from the wall.

Washable wallpaper can be sponged lightly with a mild detergent solution, then rinsed using a cloth well wrung out in clear warm water. Work from the bottom upwards.

Walls *see* CEILINGS AND WALLS; EGGSHELL, EMULSION AND GLOSS PAINT; GRASSCLOTH; HESSIAN-COVERED WALLS; SILK WALL HANGINGS; TILED SURFACES; VINYL WALLCOVERING; WALLPAPER; WOOD PANELLING.

Wicker *see* BASKETWARE AND CANE.

Windows

Windows need cleaning both inside and out if they are to transmit light and possibly a view. Cleaning is best done on a sunless day otherwise the glass dries too quickly leaving smears. Proprietary window cleaners come in liquid, trigger operated spray and aerosol form. Good ones include Windolene and SOS Glass Works. The sprays or aerosols may be easier to apply to small areas like leaded lights.

Home cleaners include a bucketful of warm water with 105ml laundry borax dissolved in it, or a small bucket of water plus 30ml vinegar. A clean chamois leather is the most effective applicator. For a really good shine, buff the dry window with a crumpled pad of newspaper – the printers' ink does a good job. Alternatively rub up with a dry chamois leather or soft cloth. A window cleaner incorporating a rubber blade is a quick way of removing the water plus dirt on large pane windows. Wipe the blade after each downward stroke.

House windows and conservatories stay clean for longer and are protected from staining and discolouration if they have been treated with Clear-Shield, a transparent, non-stick protective coating that bonds chemically to the surface of the glass. The glass can be treated in situ by licensees or supplied already treated, and the treatment will last up to five years (depending on conditions), when it can be replaced. For information and suppliers, contact Ritec (UK) Ltd., *see* ADDRESSES.

Wood

Floors

For care of both block and strip wood floors *see* FLOORS, WOOD.

Furniture

For care of antique furniture *see* ANTIQUE FURNITURE. Modern furniture may be finished with French polish (*see* FRENCH-POLISHED SURFACES), oil, paint, seal or wax.

Oiled natural wood This needs little care other than regular dusting and a sparing application of a proprietary oil about three times a year (*see also* ROSEWOOD and TEAK).

Sealed wood Apart from dusting, this just needs wiping over with a damp cloth plus an occasional application of cleaner/polish when the shine starts to disappear.

Waxed furniture should be dusted frequently and waxed and polished thoroughly from time to time, either with a proprietary product such as Antiquax or with a home-made polish (for recipe *see* ANTIQUE FURNITURE(. Be sure to apply the polish sparingly and rub really well so that a smooth patina, rather than a sticky build-up that attracts dust, is created. Fingermarks can usually be removed by rubbing briskly with a soft cloth or by wiping the surface with a cloth wrung out in a 1:8 solution of vinegar and warm water. Don't over-wet and dry off well.

Panelling

Remove dust regularly, using a brush attachment on the vacuum cleaner or long-handled brush with a soft cloth duster tied over the head.

Sealed wood panelling General cleaning is best done with a cloth wrung out in a warm, mild detergent solution. Finish with clear water and buff dry. From time to time brighten the surface with an all-purpose cleaner/polish eg Mr Sheen or Johnson Wax Free Sparkle.

Wax finished panelling This needs occasional polishing with a paste wax such as Antiquax. When the wax builds up to an unacceptable, dust-attracting level, remove it with white spirit or Antiquax Furniture Cleaner applied on a soft cloth, and repolish. Neglected panelling which is faded or scratched will be improved by rubbing over with fine steel wool dipped in white spirit, working always in the direction of the grain. Then polish and buff with a soft cloth.

Utensils

Wooden cheese and bread boards should be wiped over with a cloth wrung out in clear warm water and left to dry naturally in an airy place, standing on one edge so both large surfaces are exposed to the air.

Salad bowls should never be immersed in water but wiped out with absorbent kitchen paper and then with a cloth wrung out in clear warm water. From time to time apply a thin layer of corn oil to the wood and wipe it off thoroughly with kitchen paper. This type does not go rancid and helps to protect the wood against staining and to maintain its sheen.

Stains can often be removed by rubbing with a nylon scourer moistened in warm water along the grain. Bad marks may need to be rubbed with wet-and-dry abrasive paper. Wipe the wood first with a dry cloth to remove loose particles, then with a damp one.

Pastry boards, chopping blocks, rolling pins and wooden spoons should be washed quickly and dried so that water does not penetrate the wood and cause stains. Never soak wooden utensils. Use a firm-bristled brush and scrub in the direction of the grain to remove any food particles.

Zinc

Wash when necessary in hot soapy water. Perforated zinc, such as that found on the front of old-fashioned meat safes, should be scrubbed with warm soapy water and a soft brush, then rinsed and dried thoroughly.

4

Fabric laundering guide

Washing machines may have taken the physical drudgery out of washday, but they have not necessarily made it simpler. New developments in man-made fibres and the improvement, in 'washability' terms, of old favourites such as wool and cotton, as well as the large number of washing programmes offered by modern machines make it essential that you match the right detergent with the right termperature and washing action for your fabric.

Most clothes and household items carry a textile care label to help you launder them successfully. In 1986 the Laundry Code was revised to take into account new developments in detergent and washing machine technology. The new labels are now appearing on clothes, washing machines and detergents. However, not many of us throw away things so quickly, and will have items carrying the old labels. To help you, we have provided a chart (*see* p. 132–4) showing both the old and the new symbols and explaining their meaning.

If the label on an item tells you only the kind of material it is made from, it will help you to turn to the chart on p. 135 IDENTIFYING MAN-MADE FIBRES. This will tell you what fibre group the most popular brand names belong to, and so help you in your choice of wash programmes.

Finally, it is worth familiarizing yourself with the various kinds of detergent available. Heavy duty detergent, designed for washing machine use, contains detergent (which makes water more 'wet' by breaking it up into smaller molecules), a cleaning agent (soap or synthetic), a soil suspending agent to prevent the washed-out grime from migrating back into your clothes, and bleach. Bleach does not begin to work under about 40°C; it starts being effective between 50°C and 65°C and reaches peak performance at about 85°C. 'Biological' washing powders contain enzymes which break down protein based stains such as eggs, milk and blood. Automatic powders or liquids are formulated especially for front-loading automatic washing machines. They produce very little foam, which is unnecessary to the washing process anyway, and may impede the washing action or even cause an overflow.

Light duty detergents contain no bleach or enzymes. They may be soap based (powders or flakes) or synthetic (liquids). Use them for hand washing.

Revised textile care labelling code

Old Symbol	New Symbol	Accompanying Wording	Washing temperature	
			Machine	Hand
(1/95°)	(95)	'wash in cotton cycle/ programme' or 'wash as cotton'	very hot 95°C *normal action, rinse and spin*	hand hot 50°C
(2/60°)	(60)	'wash in cotton cycle/ programme' or 'wash as cotton'	hot 60°C *normal action, rinse and spin*	hand hot 50°C
(4/50°)	(50)	'wash in synthetics cycle/ programme' or 'wash as synthetics'	hand hot 50°C *reduced action, cold rinse, reduced spin or drip dry*	
(5/40°)	(40)	'wash in cotton cycle/ programme' or 'wash as cotton'	warm 40°C *normal action, rinse and spin*	
(6/40°)	(40)	'wash in synthetics cycle/ programme' or 'wash as synthetics'	warm 40°C *reduced action, cold rinse, reduced spin*	
(7/40°)	(40)	'wash in wool cycle/ programme' or 'wash as wool'	warm 40°C *much reduced action, normal rinse and spin*	
		Hand wash	See garment label	
		Do not wash		

Washing Temperatures

100°C	Boil	Self explanatory
95°C	Very hot	Water heated to near boiling temperature.
60°C	Hot	Hotter than the hand can bear. The temperature of water coming from many domestic hot taps.
50°C	Hand hot	As hot as the hands can bear.
40°C	Warm	Pleasantly warm to the hand.

Fabric type
Used for white cotton and linen articles without special finishes, this process provides the most vigorous wash conditions. The high water temperature and maximum agitation and spinning times ensure good whiteness and stain removal.
For cotton, linen or viscose articles without special finishes where colours are fast at 60°C. Provides vigorous wash conditions but at a temperature which maintains fast colours.
For nylon; polyester/cotton mixtures; polyester; cotton and viscose articles with special finishes; cotton/acrylic mixtures. Reduced agitation and the lower wash temperature safeguards the finish and colour. Cold rinsing followed by short spinning minimises creases.
Suited to cotton, linen and viscose articles where colours are fast at 40°C but not at 60°C. This process ensures thorough cleansing but at the lower wash temperature essential to safeguard colour fastness.
For those articles which require gentle, low temperature laundering to preserve colour and shape and minimise creasing eg acrylics; acetate and triacetate, including mixtures with wool; polyester/wool blends.
For wool, including blankets, wool mixed with other fibres, and silk, requiring low temperature washing with minimum agitation. This treatment preserves colour, size and handle. Do not rub or hand wring.

Include articles with Programme 3 60°C care label in [50]

Include articles with Programme 8 30°C care label in [40] or [40]

Significance of the Bar underneath the Wash Tub

Absence of bar [⎵] denotes normal (maximum) machine action and is labelled 'wash as cotton'

A bar [⎵_] denotes reduced (medium) machine action and is labelled 'wash as synthetics'.

A broken bar [⎵ _ _] denotes much reduced (minimum) wash action and labelled 'wash as wool'.

Mixing Wash Loads

You can mix wash labels without a bar provided you wash at the lowest temperature shown.

You can mix wash labels with and without a bar provided that you wash at the lowest temperature, BUT you must reduce the wash action.

Articles with [40] must be washed as wool at a much reduced wash action.

'Wash separately' means what it says.

Bleaching
This symbol indicates that household (chlorine) bleach could be used. Care must be taken to follow the manufacturer's instructions.

When this symbol appears on a label household bleach must *not* be used.

Ironing
The number of dots in the ironing symbol indicates the correct temperature setting – the fewer the dots the cooler the iron setting.

cool   warm   hot   do not iron

Dry Cleaning
The letter in the circle refers to the solvent which may be used in the dry-cleaning process, and those using 'coin op' dry-cleaning should check that the cleaning symbol shown on the label is the same as that in the instructions given on the front of the machine.

Goods normal for dry-cleaning in all solvents.

Goods normal for dry-cleaning in perchloroethylene, white spirit, Solvent 113 and Solvent 11.

Goods normal for dry-cleaning in white spirit or Solvent 113.

Do not dry-clean.

N.B. When the circle containing P or F is underlined, do not 'coin op' clean, as this indicates that these materials are sensitive to dry cleaning and require special treatment.

Drying
Care labels may also include one or other of the following symbols recommending a particular drying method.

Tumble dry on a low heat setting.

Tumble dry on a high heat setting.

Do not tumble dry.

Where the prohibition symbol above is used, further instructions, such as 'dry flat' for heavy knitted garments, should be given in words.

IDENTIFYING MAN-MADE FIBRES

Fibre Brand Names	Man-made Fibre Group	Fibre-Brand Names	Man-Made Fibre Group
Dicel	ACETATE	Dacron	
		Diolen	
Acrilan		Fortrel	
Courtelle		Mitrelle	
Dolan	ACRYLIC	Quallofil	POLYESTER
Dralon		Tergal	
Orlon		Terinda	
		Terlenka	
Lycra	ELASTANE	Terylene	
		Trevira	
Lurex	METALLIC		
Acrilan SEF	MODACRYLIC	Meraklon	POLYPROPYLENE
Kanekalon	(Flame retard-		
Teklan	ant properties)	Arnel	TRIACETATE
		Tricel	
Antron			
Bri-nylon		Danufil	
Cantrece		Danuflor	
Enka Nylon		Durafil	
Enka Perlon		Evlan	VISCOSE
Qazul	NYLON	Fibro	
Quintesse	(POLYAMIDE)	Sarille	
Tactel		Viloft	
Tactesse			
Tendrelle			
Timbrelle			

Note: Some items of clothing and household textiles/articles may carry a fibre content label indicating the fibre group, eg acetate, nylon, instead of the brand name of the fibre.

Addresses

Acid-free tissue, card and boxes   Atlantis Paper Co. Ltd., Gulliver's Wharf, 105 Wapping Lane, London E1 9RW 01-481 3784.

Antiquax products   Antique shops or hardware stores. In case of difficulty, write to: James Briggs Ltd., Salmon Fields, Royton, Oldham OL2 6HZ.

Bell products   Available by post from A. Bell & Co. Ltd., Kingsthorpe, Northampton NN2 6LT 0604 712505.

Belsealer   See entry for Bell products.

Betterware Kitchen Carbon Remover   Details of local agent from Betterware Sales Ltd., Fairview Estate, Kingsbury Road, Curdworth, Sutton Coldfield, W. Midlands B76 9EH 0675 70094.

Bissell carpet and upholstery cleaning products   Large department and hardware stores. Larger Co-op stores.

Brummer Stopping   Small DIY and handyman shops.

Cee Bee Hide Food   Good leather shops. If no local stockist, contact Connolly Bros. Ltd., Wandle Bank, Wimbledon, London SW19 1DW 01-543 4611.

Celmac products   Celmac Products Ltd., Victoria Works, Saxon Street, Denton, Manchester M34 3AB 061 336 4401 will supply details of your nearest stockist.

Chempro T   Boots' larger branches, also hardware stores displaying the STERMAT sign.

CP-60   All branches of B & Q.

Cuprinol Teak Oil   from stockists of Cuprinol products, such as DIY shops. If no local stockist, contact Cuprinol Ltd., Adderwell, Frome, Somerset BA11 1NL.

Dax Chemical Brass Tarnish & Verdigris Remover   Dax Products Ltd., PO Box 119, Nottingham 0602 609996.

Descalite products   Hardware stores. In case of difficulty, contact Descalite Chemical Supply Co., 30 Swale Road, Strood, Kent ME2 2TT 0322 58887.

Dri Gear   Stocked at all branches of Camping & Outdoor Centres. In case of difficulty, write to: Scout Shops Ltd., Churchill Industrial Estate, Lancing, W. Sussex BN15 8UG.

Dylon products   Department stores, chemists, major multiples and grocery outlets.

Evo-Stik Adhesive Cleaner (191)   Evode Ltd., Common Road, Stafford, Staffs ST16 3EH.

Fortificuir   Obtainable direct from Alfred Maltby & Son Ltd., 28–30 St Michael's Street, Oxford, OX1 2EB.

Frank Odell Barbecue Cleaner   B & Q, Texas Homecare, major garden centres.

Fungo   Dax Products Ltd., PO Box 119, Nottingham O602 609996.

Furmoto products   Hardware stores, or direct from The Sales, Dept., Kent Chemicals, George House, Bridewell Lane, Tenterden, Kent TN30 6HS.

Goddard's Jewellery Care Kit   Jewellery section of department stores, jewellers, silversmiths and some hardware stores and grocers.

Goddard's Long Term Silver Cloth   See above.

Greendale Carpet and Fabric Spot'N'Stain Removal Kit   Carpet Stockholding (Green Group) Ltd., Penn House, Penn Broad Street, Hereford HR4 9AP 0432 354201.

Handy Andy   Independent grocers, branches of Londis.

Hidelife   Available from most leather furniture retailers. In case of difficulty, contact Bridge of Weir Leather Co., Clydesdale Works, Bridge of Weir, Renfrewshire, Scotland PA11 3LF 0505 612132.

Holts Anti-Mist   Most car accessory shops. In case of difficulty, write to: Holt Products Ltd., Lloyds House, Alderley Road, Wilmslow, Cheshire SK9 8QT for details of your nearest stockist.

Humbrol's Universal Cleaner   for removing model making cement (polystyrene cement). Through model shops and DIY shops.

Izal Bath Cleaner   Hardware stores, department stores and some general stores.

Jenolite Bath Stain Remover   Through most branches of Boots and hardware stores. In case of difficulty, write to Jenolite, Rusham Road, Egham, Surrey TW20 9SL.

Jenolite Rust Remover & Preventer   Halfords and hardware stores.

Jif   Supermarkets.

Johnson products (other than Traffic Wax)   Hardware shops, supermarkets, some department stores, larger branches of Boots.

Johnson Traffic Wax Liquid   Only available in 5 litre quantity. For address of nearest distributor, contact Consumer Advisory Service, Johnson Wax Ltd., Frimley Green, Camberley, Surrey GU16 5AJ 0276 63456.

Joy products   DIY shops, hardware shops and paint shops. In case of difficulty contact Hunting Lubricants and Specialised Products Ltd., 0532 492820.

Keyline Chewing Gum Remover   By post from Keyline, PO Box 167, Earl's Barton, Northamptonshire NN6 0ER 0604 812155.

Kleeneze products   Only available through Kleeneze agent, contact head office to ask an agent to call: Kleeneze Ltd., Service Department, Hanham, Bristol BS15 3DY 0272 670861.

Kleenoff Drain Cleaner   Branches of Boots, hardware stores.

Klenzene   All enquiries to: Gestetner Ltd., 210 Euston Road, London NW1 01 387 7021

K2R Stain Remover Spray   Chemists, department stores and some major supermarkets.

Kurust   Car accessory shops.

Leather Groom   See entry for Swade products.

Liberon products   Independent ironmongers and hardware stores.

Mangers products   Woolworths, Sainsburys Homebase and Co-op stores.

Manor House Decanter Drier   by post from Hurley Style Ltd., The Manor House, Hurley, Berkshire SL6 5NB 0628 824303.

Marley Floor Cleaner   Hardware shops, department stores and supermarkets.

Meltonian products   Most shoe shops; shoe section of department stores.

Microwave Clean   Tesco supermarkets, Sainsburys, John Lewis Partnership stores.

Movol   Chemists and major department stores.

Mystox LPL   Picreator Enterprises Ltd., 44 Park View Gardens, Hendon, London NW4 2PN

1001 products   Most supermarkets and hardware stores.

Oz products   Chemists, hardware shops, some department stores, some supermarkets.

Parker Inks (solvents for)   Enquiries to: Parker Pen Company Ltd., Service Department, PO Box 6, Newhaven, East Sussex BN9 OAU. Information and leaflets are available.

Punch products   Branches of Peter Lord, Barratts, Tandem, Timpson, Mr Minit and Automagic. *Punch Salt Stain Remover* also stocked by Tesco Supermarkets.

Renaissance Wax Polish   Picreator Enterprises Ltd., 44 Park View Gardens, Hendon, London NW4 2PN.

Rentokil products   DIY shops, hardware stores, John Lewis Partnership stores.

Ritec (UK) Ltd.   15 Royal London Estate, West Road, London, N17 OXL 01 885 5155

Ronseal products   DIY shops, hardware stores and some supermarkets.

Ronuk Wax Polish   John Lewis Partnership stores, Waitrose supermarkets, hardware and grocery stores.

Rustin's products   DIY shops, paint shops and some department stores.

Sabco Carpet and Upholstery Shampoo   House of Fraser stores, Co-op stores.

ServiceMaster First Aid Kit   For carpets and upholstery. Obtainable through local ServiceMaster Associates (see Yellow Pages). In case of difficulty, write to: ServiceMaster Ltd., 50 Commercial Square, Freemans Common, Leicester LE2 7SR.

Scale Away   Grocery and hardware stores, drugstores, Asda and larger branches of Boots.

Scotchgard Fabric Protector   John Lewis stores, Tesco supermarkets.

Scotchgard Suede and Leather Protector   Lilley & Skinner, Dolcis, Saxone, Barratt and Olwen shoe shops.

Scotchgard Treatment   applied by Scotchgard licensed applicators. For your nearest dealer dial 100 and ask for Freephone 1002.

Shaws products   Pet shops and pet sections of department stores.

Solvol Autosol   Car accessory shops.

SOS products   in case of difficulty, contact Bayer UK Ltd., Consumer Products Division, Bayer House, Newbury, Berkshire RG13 1JA 0635 39000.

Spotkleen Stain Removing Cloth   Branches of John Lewis, Fortnum and Mason.

Stain Devils Stain Removers   Chemists, hardware shops, some department stores, some supermarkets.

Stain Slayer   Chemists, hardware shops, Robert Dyas, John Lewis, camping and caravanning suppliers.

Stephensons Olde English Furniture Cream   Harrods, Selfridges, Robert Dyas Group, Stern-Osmat Group, Nurdin & Peacock cash and carry.

Strypit   See entry for Rustin's products.

Swade products   Leather and sheepskin retail outlets. Department stores including John Lewis, Harrods, Selfridges.

Swarfega Hand Cleanser   Car accessory shops such as Halfords, also branches of Boots, large supermarkets and some hardware stores.

3-in-One products   Halfords, B & Q, Woolworths and leading hardware stores.

Translac Polyurethane Clear Varnish   See entry for Ronseal.

Treasure Gold   See entry for Winsor & Newton's products.

Turtle Wax products   B & Q, Charlie Brown Auto Centres. Upholstery cleaner also available from Asda and Gateway stores.

Uniglan   Available by post from Uniglan Ltd., Hadston Industrial Estate, Hadston, Morpeth, Northumberland NE65 9YG 0670 760082.

Vanish stain removing bar   Major supermarkets and chemists.
Vilene Iron Cleaner   Haberdashery departments, Woolworths, supermarkets with a 'Sewing Centre' section and larger electrical and hardware shops.
Vim   Independent grocers, branches of Londis.

WD-40   Car accessory shops, hardware shops, DIY.
Wenol Metal Polish   John Lewis Partnership stores. Tesco supermarkets.
Winsol Paint Remover and Solvent   see entry for Winsor & Newton.
Winsor & Newton products   Art and graphics shops. Winsor & Newton, Whitefriars Avenue, Harrow, Middlesex HA3 5RH.

Organisations
Association of British Laundry, Cleaning & Rental Services Ltd.,   7 Churchill Court, 58 Station Road, North Harrow, Middlesex HA2 7SA 01 863 7755. The Drycleaning Information Bureau 01 863 8658 and the Laundry Information Bureau 01 863 9178 will give free advice about cleaning services.
The Royal School of Needlework   5, King St, London WC2E 8HN 01 240 3186. Phone or write for information.
Victoria & Albert Museum,   Exhibition Road, London SW7.
VEDC (Vitreous Enamel Development Council) Ltd.,   New House, High Street, Ticehurst, Wadhurst, Sussex TN5 7AL.

Index

Absorbed stains 13
Acetic acid 17
Acid free tissue paper 99, 108
Acrylic 62
　　baths 62, 66–67
　　paint 22
　　sinks 119
Adhesives 19–20
Alkyd paint 22
Aluminium 63
　　cookware 63
　　frame furniture 94
　　teapots 63
　　wall tiles 123
Amethysts 100
Ammonia 9, 15, 25, 44, 50, 58–9, 111
Amyl acetate 9, 17, 20
Antique
　　furniture 63–4
　　ivory 99
　　lace 102
Araldite 19
Artwipes 22
Asphalt surfaces 27

Bedlinen
　　blood on 25
　　chocolate on 27
　　cocoa on 29
　　rubber hot water bottle stain on 51
　　urine on 21, 58
　　vomit on 21, 59
Beeswax 64
Bicarbonate of soda 25, 62, 87, 116, 121
Biological washing powder 16, 30, 32,
　　39, 43, 45, 57, 58, 59, 79, 111
Blankets 67–8

electric 68
tea on 56
Bleach 24, 35, 41, 46, 61, 82, 84, 92
Blinds, canvas 71
Blotting paper 26–7, 35
Bookworm 68
Borax 16–17, 24, 27, 28, 31, 42–3, 52–3,
　　56–7, 61, 63, 66, 94, 128
Bostik No 1 19
Brickwork
　　fireplaces 83–4
　　flooring 69
　　smoke and soot on 54
Brooms 70
Buckram lampshades 103
Built-up stains 13
Burnt pans 111

Carbon steel knife blades 101
Carpet rake 71
Carpets 71–2
　　adhesives on 19–20
　　beer on 23
　　bird droppings on 24
　　blood on 25
　　candle wax on 26
　　chewing gum on 27
　　chocolate on 28
　　cocoa on 28
　　cod liver oil on 29
　　coffee on 30
　　curry on 31
　　egg on 32
　　excreta on 20
　　fats on 33
　　fountain pen ink on 41
　　fruit juice on 36

gin on 37
gravy on 38
grease on 33
henna on 39
ice cream on 39
iodine on 42
jam on 42
ketchup on 43
lipstick on 43
marmalade on 42
metal polish on 45
milk on 47
mud on 47
nail varnish on 48
oil on 33
paint on 49
paraffin oil on 50
plasticine on 51
rust marks on 52
scorch marks on 52
shoe polish on 54
soot on 54
soup on 55
stain removal from, general 14–15
tar on 55
tea on 56
Tipp-Ex on 57
urine on 20, 58
vomit on 20, 59
wine on 59

Cedar wood 93
Cellulose thinners 9, 17, 19, 20, 69
Chamois leather 104
Compound stains 13
Cooking pans
    aluminium 63
    stainless steel 120
Copydex 20
Cricket flannels 37–8
Crystal glass 95
Cut glass 95

Cutlery
    carbon steel 101
    ivory handled 99
    mother of pearl handled 109
    stainless steel 120

Desk tops, leather 105
Diamonds 100
Disinfectant 45
Dralon 47, 125, 126
Drawers, sticking 92
Dried stains 14
Drip marks on bath/sink 23

Electric blankets 68
Emeralds 100
Enzyme washing powder see
    Biological washing powder
Epoxy resin 19
Eucalyptus oil 31, 105
Evo-Stik 19
Excreta (animal) 20–21

Fake leather 105
Fireclay sinks 119
First aid for stains 11–12
Foam baths 67
Formica 102
French chalk 33

Garden ornaments, lead 104
Glass fibre baths 67
Glasspaper 62, 91, 92
Gloves, leather 105
Glycerine 17, 29, 31, 50, 52, 55, 60, 68,
    117

Hairbrush 70
    ivory 99
    tortoiseshell 124
Handbags
    canvas 71

leather 33, 45, 106
  plastic 40, 41
  suede 40
Hands
  henna stains on 39
  tobacco stains on 57
Hard water marks
  on baths 23, 66
Hinges, sticking 92
Hot water bottles, rubber 51
Humbrol polystyrene cement 20
Humidifier 64
Hydrogen peroxide 14, 24, 25, 31, 40,
  46, 53, 56, 59, 61

Imitation tortoiseshell 124
Indelible lipstick 43
Iroko 93
Ivory
  antique 33
  hairbrushes 99
  handmirrors 98
  knife holders 99
  piano keys 112

Lampshades 103
  buckram 103
  plastic 35, 103
  vellum 35, 103
Lacquered brass 69
Latex adhesive 20
Laundry borax *see* Borax
Leaf shiner 97
Leather 104–107
  books 68
  desk tops 105
  handbags 106
    fats, grease and oil on 33
    mildew on 45
  gloves 105
  shoes 106
    fats, grease and oil on 33

  mildew on 45
  rain spots on 51
  salt water marks on 52
  tar on 55
  urine on 58
luggage 105
upholstery 105
  fat, grease and oil on 33
  mildew on 45
Lemon juice 41, 42, 52, 119
  and salt paste 69
Lemon, squeezed 39
Lighter fuel 9, 17, 31, 34, 51
Luggage, leather 105
  mildew on 45

Man-made fibre chart 135
Marcasite jewellery 100
Mattresses 106
  blood on 25
  urine on 58
  vomit on 59
Melinex 109
Methylated spirits 9, 17, 22, 26–27, 32,
  33, 37, 39, 40, 41, 43, 45, 49, 53, 54,
  60, 111, 112
Modelmaking cement 20

Nail varnish remover 9, 17, 20, 69, 102
Net curtains 79, 102
Non-stick bakeware 63, 65, 110

Oil paint 22
Opals 100
Ovens 75
  doors 76
  shelves 76
Oven-to-table ware 95

Paint brushes 70
Panelling, wood
  sealed wood 129

wax finished wood 129
Patent leather 105
Pearls 100
Petroleum jelly 73
Perstorp Warerite 102
Photographic hypo 42
Poster paint 22
Powder paint 22
Pre-wash laundry aids 17

Rubies 100
Rust marks
  on baths 23
  on carpets 52
  on steel 121

Salad bowls, wooden 129
Salt and lemon juice paste 69
Sapphires 100
Scuff marks
  on linoleum 86
  on rubber floors 86
  on vinyl floors 87
Shower heads 117
Silver polish, homemade 118
Sodium hydrosulphite 41
Spirits of salts 9, 54
Steam cleaners for carpets 72
Steel wool 69, 74, 75, 86, 89, 98, 99
Sticky labels 20
Stoved enamel 82
Suede 106
  clothes
    fats, grease and oil on 34
    rain spots on 51
  handbags
    ballpoint pen on 40
  shoes
    fats, grease and oil on 34
    rain spots on 51
    salt water marks on 52
    tar on 55

urine on 58

Taps, chrome 74
Teak 93
Teapots 121–122
  aluminium 63
Textile Care Labelling Codes 132–134
Tide marks 23
Tubular furniture
  chrome 74
  steel 94
Turpentine 9, 17, 64, 70, 95, 104, 113
Turquoises 100

Unidentified stains 14
Upholstery 124–125
  adhesives on 19–20
  beer on 24
  ball point pen on 40
  bird droppings on 24
  blood on 25
  candle wax on 26
  chewing gum on 27
  cocoa on 29
  coffee on 30
  curry on 31
  duplicating ink on 31
  dyes on 32
  egg on 32
  fat on 33
  felt tip on 40–41
  fly specks on 35
  foundation cream on 36
  fountain pen ink on 41
  fruit juice on 36
  gin on 37
  gravy on 38
  grease on 33
  henna on 39
  ice cream on 39
  jam on 42
  ketchup on 43

lipstick on 43
marmalade on 42
mayonnaise on 45
metal polish on 45
mildew on 45
milk on 47
mud on 47
mustard on 48
nail varnish on 48
paint on 49–50
paraffin on 50
perspiration on 50
plasticine on 51
rust marks on 52
scorch marks on 52
shellac on 53
shoe polish on 52
soup on 55
tar on 55
tea on 57
urine on 21, 58
vomit on 21
wine on 60
Utensils
  acrylic 62
  aluminium 63
  enamel 82
  cast iron 72
  stainless steel 120
  tin 124
  wood 129

Vases, flower 35

Vellum 125
  lampshades 35, 103
Vinegar, malt 84
  white *see* White vinegar
Vinyl 126
  dolls
    ballpoint on 40
    felt tip on 41
  floors 86–87
  headboards
    hair oil on 38
    felt tip on 41
  upholstery 125
  wallpaper/covering 126
    candle wax on 26
    crayon on 30

Wallpaper 126
  candle wax on 26
  crayon on 30
  fat, grease and oil on 35
  hair oil on 38
  lipstick on 44
Watercolour paint 22
Wet-and-dry paper 62, 130, 101
White vinegar 24, 51, 64, 86, 119, 120, 123
  and ammonia solution 106
  and salt solution 69, 79
  and water solution 113, 116, 124, 128
White spirit 9, 17, 22, 23, 45, 49, 87, 129
Woodworm 68